YOU'RE SENDING ME WHERE?

ALSO BY ERIC DREGNI

Published by the University of Minnesota Press

By the Waters of Minnetonka

In Cod We Trust: Living the Norwegian Dream

Let's Go Fishing! Fish Tales from the North Woods

Midwest Marvels: Roadside Attractions across Iowa, Minnesota, the Dakotas, and Wisconsin

Minnesota Marvels: Roadside Attractions in the Land of Lakes

Never Trust a Thin Cook and Other Lessons from Italy's Culinary Capital

Vikings in the Attic: In Search of Nordic America

YOU'RE SENDING ME **WHERE?**

DISPATCHES FROM SUMMER CAMP

ERIC DREGNI

UNIVERSITY OF MINNESOTA PRESS

Minneapolis • London

Names were changed to avoid confusion and protect the guilty. The chronology of events over the past ten years was altered slightly for narrative flow. —E. D.

Copyright 2017 by Eric Dregni

Published by the University of Minnesota Press
111 Third Avenue South, Suite 290
Minneapolis, MN 55401-2520
http://www.upress.umn.edu

Design and production by Mighty Media, Inc.
Interior and text design by Chris Long

ISBN 978-1-5179-0240-7
A Cataloging-in-Publication record for this book is available from the Library of Congress.

Printed in the United States of America on acid-free paper

The University of Minnesota is an equal-opportunity educator and employer.

22 21 20 19 18 17   10 9 8 7 6 5 4 3 2 1

To my Mom,
who pushed me on that damn bus
and started this adventure

CONTENTS

WHAT DID I DO TO DESERVE THIS?

NATIONWIDE, MORE THAN FOURTEEN MILLION KIDS ATTEND summer camps annually, and growing up, I was determined not to be one of them. I'd heard the whole shtick of how "this will be good for you" and how rich kids, poor kids, and anyone who goes will benefit. This was back before the word *camp* had been co-opted to mean any kids' summer activity—because, really, who wants to attend "summer school" when we can go to *camp*?

I knew that camp took place in the woods, away from all the creature comforts we have at home (especially today, when kids can't tear their eyes from mesmerizing rectangular screens). Nowadays, camps lure kids by offering everything from hockey to volleyball, yoga to sewing, even circus and computer themes. When I was a kid, pretty much my only option was YMCA wilderness camp. My mom wanted me to escape the summer doldrums and experience all the beauty of the north woods. She had been on the first girls' canoe trip at the remote Camp Menogyn in the Boundary Waters in the 1950s, so her six-year-old son could at the very least go to a comfy day camp for a few days. I wanted nothing to do with it.

Despite my refusal, she signed me up. On my first day of camp my mom hugged me good-bye, and I refused to get on that damn bus. No way. My arms and legs splayed out and grabbed the frame of the door as she shoved me forward. Why should I give up the safety of our suburban home to be sent into the jungle where ferocious beasts were eager to eat me?

I screamed, and the entire busload of kids watched the scene in horror, perhaps thinking that they would be tortured as well. My mom stopped pushing for a moment, and I tried to make a break for it. Instead, she grabbed me and put me on the step of the bus as the driver quickly shut the door. Tears trailed down my cheeks as I banged on the door trying to escape, but the bus driver jammed the stick shift into gear, and a cloud of smoke puffed behind the bus. My mother had abandoned me, and she grew smaller and smaller in the distance as the bus whisked me off as a prisoner to Camp Christmas Tree.

This first day of camp was the worst experience in my life. Why had I been abandoned by my parents and shipped off to this prison to be eaten alive by bears, wolves, or cougars? If they didn't eat me, I'd surely have my blood drained drop by drop by buzzing mosquitoes puncturing my sunburned skin. Then there were bats, spiders, ticks, poison ivy . . . What did I do to deserve this?

When the bus returned me later that evening, I chose not to remember the scene I had caused in the morning that made my mom feel ill for the rest of the day. I was transformed, brainwashed. Hooked. Just like for millions of other little campers, the worst day of my life had become the best one. I no longer dreaded the outdoors but knew that if I put on enough bug spray and sun cream, I would survive and thrive at camp. I remembered the mirror lakes reflecting the puffy rabbit-shaped clouds, and the pair of loons who crooned just for me. I longed to be filthy from rolling down hills, dizzy from climbing trees, fearless when starting campfires, and dangerous with my big stick ready to take down any bears that attacked.

Over the years and decades, I veered from outdoor adventures to a foreign language camp in the wilderness, one of fifteen such camps in northern Minnesota. If life at a wilderness camp isn't crazy enough, just add Italians to the mix. For ten years, I have watched the kids get off the bus in culture shock and suffering gut-wrenching homesickness. I was once one of the kids, and now I am a camp director.

Ever since that first painful day, I knew that camp was for me.

FOXFIRE

AT NINE YEARS OLD, I WAS PRETTY SURE THAT I COULD TAME nature. I had a bow with a quiver full of arrows and a belt to carry a small pickax and a leather case for a deadly sharp fishing knife— none of which my parents let me carry to camp. Still, I signed up for a two-week overnight session deep in the woods of rural Wisconsin. The second night we had a massive game of capture the flag on all of the forty-acre island. Kids ran everywhere but usually stayed close to the center of camp. My cabinmates and I took a different path. Sneaking through the underbrush—and probably poison ivy—we searched for the flag and got hopelessly lost. If a bear attacked, I had none of my weapons to take it down. Our disgruntled counselors mounted a search party to bring us in from the cold. We had just started our overnight camp, and already events had turned sour.

Nick, our nineteen-year-old counselor who already had a full beard, convinced our assistant counselor, Dan, that our group of nine-year-olds was the "bad cabin" since we respected no boundaries or our counselors. Dan was just seventeen and obviously wanted to chase girls rather than be shackled with needy boys who refused to bathe. We figured our smell would keep away the wild animals—and girls. Reasoning that we would fall in line out in the deep, dark woods, Nick and Dan took us out on a three-day canoe trip. After haplessly zigzagging across the lake, we found a campsite. The counselors wanted to "get back to basics" by relaxing in the sun and going skinny-dipping. They correctly figured that we timid preteens wanted nothing to do with nudity, so we began setting up the tents while the counselors sunbathed naked in the warm sun next to the lake.

What they didn't count on was that little Rob would find the hatchet hidden deep in the food sack. He bragged how his dad would take him hunting and so he knew how to survive in the wilderness, just like Grizzly Adams. We stood back as he swung the small ax like a berserker Viking trying to cut down trees. When that proved tiresome, he chopped at stones to watch sparks fly. The chipped hatchet was soon dull as a hammer, but he said his weapon made him king of our tribe.

Then Johnny, the kid with the "Let's Boogie" T-shirt who carried dog-eared photos of his beer can collection, discovered a box of matches. He wanted to make s'mores, but Alex, the "husky" kid in desperate need of a belt to hike up his jeans, had already finished off the Hershey's chocolate bars. Alex's hand was deep into the marshmallows when I snatched the sack from his grasp—we could at least roast them over a campfire.

Despite using nearly the whole box of matches, Johnny couldn't keep the flames alive. We had no paper, so for some reason he tried to burn the tent rope, which smoldered into a useless mass. He liked the dizzying effect of breathing in the fumes. Meanwhile, Rob kept busy covering every inch of his body with bug spray, and Johnny discovered that Deep Woods Off! is highly flammable. He held up a match and simply sprayed toward the logs in the fire pit. A huge flame emitted from the aerosol can and singed the hair on his hands. Some kids impaled marshmallows on sharpened green sticks to roast with Johnny's makeshift flamethrower. Johnny used up all of his bug spray, but the logs finally sizzled to life. We applauded Johnny's inventive camping skills.

As we feasted on marshmallows cooked with flaming insecticide, the counselors ventured back from the beach, drawn by the bizarre smell of burning chemicals and caramelized sugar. Nick and Dan finally put on clothes and admired the blaze Johnny had started, but they grabbed the hatchet from Rob, who had chopped off every low-hanging branch he could reach. Just as they noticed the molten mass of rope that we needed to set up the tents properly, Johnny tossed his used-up can of Off! on the fire.

"Get down!" Nick yelled. "This could blow!" We ran away from the fire and ducked behind the trees twenty feet away. Nick grabbed the griddle to use as a shield and slowly approached the fire. Despite our fear, we were all awed by the impressive BOOM of the exploding aerosol can and the ensuing mini mushroom cloud. I can't say, though, that it stopped us from wanting more. Johnny and Alex tossed their cans of bug spray into the flames, hoping for more fireworks. Nick ducked and crept up on the other cans with his cooking pan armor and put a kettle on his head as a helmet. Looking like a knight with a lance, he poked at the fire with a long stick and scooted the remaining aerosol cans out of the flames.

We cheered, but Nick and Dan gave us fierce looks in return. We knew we'd pay for our tricks, so they put us on dinner duty. We obediently cut carrots, potatoes, and chunks of beef to wrap in tinfoil to make "hobo dinner," which inevitably made for overcooked meat and miserably underdone potatoes. We sat in silence, hoping the counselors would cheer up, and no one except Alex enjoyed the dismal meal, including scorched bannock bread. Rob, Johnny, and I volunteered to clean up to get away from the awful counselors, but we didn't know how to do the dishes. I timidly asked Dan how we should wash the plates.

"Just go to the lake and wash them!" he growled.

The three of us went down to the shore, dutifully put on our life jackets, and placed all the metal dishes in the canoe. We hopped in the boat and paddled out a good fifty yards into the lake to get away from the sand of the shore. We washed the plates off the side of the canoe and, as good environmentalists, tried to use as little soap as possible to avoid polluting the lake. We watched as the dishes sank out of sight down to the bottom of the lake. At first we laughed, but then when they didn't rise to the surface, we knew we were now in real trouble. We considered escaping back to our cabin rather than returning to the campsite but knew that would be far worse.

Instead, we returned to tell our counselors that they had given us terrible advice to wash the plates in the middle of the lake. Nick and Dan didn't believe us at first but then understood that we truly were that stupid. When the screaming stopped (they vowed to make our parents pay for those apparently valuable dishes), they told us it was time for some good ghost stories. We should have pleasantly declined and gone to bed.

The sun's last orange rays crept through the trees to be replaced by the flickering glow of the campfire. We could no longer have bug spray, especially near the fire, since the counselors strangely didn't like the fireworks. We noticed black shadows flittering on the trees behind us, like spirits haunting the woods to terrify naughty kids, but realized these were just our shadows from the flames. Dan tried to scare us with the tale of the vanishing hitchhiker with a hook for an arm, but what made us shiver were the true stories of the Wisconsin legend Ed Gein. We learned how he dug up corpses to make lampshades and was always in search of fresh campers to eat. They described his little shack on the other side of Lake Wapogasset, where he would hide when he escaped the insane asylum. (Only later did we learn that his house was many miles to the north and not on a lake. In fact, the only danger on the other side of the lake was a Lutheran Bible camp.)

Nick and Dan had their revenge. Even if we thought we were kings of the jungle, we were no match for ghost stories, especially real ones. With our teeth chattering, Nick and Dan ordered us to follow them into the woods. We quickly obeyed because who would want to stay next to the campfire and become a snack for Ed Gein? Dan stopped Rob from grabbing the hatchet, so the camper instead snatched a branch to club any psychos on the loose. Nick told us to get our pillowcases and prepare for a snipe hunt in the woods. None of us knew what a snipe was, and we wondered if this was some sort of payback for the rest of the day. Nick explained, "Snipe are delicious birds that only come out at night."

"So we're supposed to catch a wild bird and then eat it?" Alex asked. "I'd rather eat s'mores."

Nick ignored his pragmatism and explained to us that we were going to have a good adventure. "That sounds like a terrible idea," Johnny said.

Nick insisted, "Now that it's dark, you shine your flashlight in their eyes, which stuns them for a minute. Then you grab them in your pillowcase." We wandered through the woods in the dark, blinding each other with flashlights as we made sure Ed Gein hadn't infiltrated our group. Dan dashed away from the group into the woods and shouted that he'd seen one. He then showed us that the snipe had nibbled a hole in his pillowcase to escape. We all examined our own pillowcases to make sure they were secure enough to hold a snipe. I wondered if we were going about this all wrong since cotton cloth obviously wouldn't properly hold a healthy snipe. Besides, did I really want to catch a live bird? Suddenly, Rob, Johnny, and the others saw snipes everywhere and jumped at them, disappearing with the counselors into the woods. I was left alone with a dying battery in my flashlight.

Darkness enveloped me. I saw no way out and couldn't hear the shouting anymore. If I began walking, I could go the wrong direction and end up lost forever. Should I just sleep where I was and wait till dawn? I had no tools to subdue nature, only my pillowcase and a dead flashlight. Slowly my eyes adjusted to the night, and I could see. I was cloaked in a sea of blackness that seeped into every pore, but I felt protected. Ed Gein or other evil creatures of the night couldn't touch me because the woods sheltered me. I looked down and saw a green stick, glowing as if it were some sort of magical sword. I remembered hearing the legends about enchanted foxfire illuminated by phosphorescent fungi. I grabbed the stick, using it to light the path back to the tents.

The rest of the campers had since returned and hadn't noticed that anyone was missing. They roasted marshmallows over a fire of wood, not aerosol cans, as I showed them my torch of foxfire. The kids wondered what sort of devil's work I'd discovered from the demons of the woods. Rob touched the foxfire nervously, expecting to be burned. Johnny wanted to brown his marshmallow by its light and to set the stick on fire to see if it would explode. Alex tried to eat it. Even the counselors were impressed, or perhaps they were satisfied that they'd tricked us into a mythical snipe hunt, even though none of us actually believed we would catch a bird in a sack, gut it, skin it, and roast it over a fire. Besides, the darkness would surely protect the snipe.

THE RIVER THAT WASN'T THERE

By the time I turned thirteen, I was ready to become a "pioneer," the highest level of camper at the Wisconsin camp I had been attending for several years. My older brother Michael had led pioneers on some intense canoe trips on the remote rivers of Wisconsin—the Flambeau, Namekagon, and the Upper Saint Croix—which French voyageurs charted as many as three hundred years ago but are still wild riverways. The groups of teenagers that my brother led were free from their parents and did dangerous things like run rapids through churning waters, and he even told me about how they jumped from bridges into the river. In the end, they were tougher, changed by the wilderness.

As a camper, I couldn't have my brother as a counselor for a trip down the famous Flambeau, so my brother's best friend, Phil, led our group of eight boys. Everyone loved Phil, who was tall with big biceps and a friendly smile. He convinced our group that we were tough enough to paddle the far-off upper Totagatic River. No other trip had dared go down this river, but Phil deemed us the chosen ones. We cheered at the thought of this great adventure. Myths passed down through generations told that the Ojibwe spirit of Wanabuju haunted the Totagatic and would make thunderous sounds to ward off intruders. Around the river, remote copper mines now stood abandoned, and only an occasional logging road wiggled up into the territory. Along one of these roads paralleling the river, a man named Blackburn built a logging shack in the 1890s, but the site is now forever haunted by the ghosts of a brutal ax murder. Legend said that gold was buried somewhere on the spot. Phil warned us that if we committed to this trip, we might not see any sign of civilization for the entire ten-day trip.

Phil and the assistant counselor, BJ, showed us the map of this wild river, whose whitewater was classified as high as IV out of VI in difficulty, which meant that we would have to portage around the nearly impassable IV rapids and scout the level III ones from shore before shooting them in the canoes. We studied the maps, and my brother Michael confirmed that these looked like the best rapids in all of Wisconsin. We packed up our forty- to fifty-pound Duluth packs, which we would tie to the canoes so we didn't lose them in case we capsized in the river. We were too young to have seen the movie *Deliverance* but had heard all about what could happen on wild rivers in remote woods. In the age before cell phones, we had to rely on our own knowledge of the woods to survive. Phil packed the first-aid kit in an old olive-green military ammunition box with a dime taped inside to make a call in case of an emergency—if we could even find a phone. We had to prepare for anything.

The night before we left on the ten-day trip, we slept nervously on the wooden floors of the platform tents on the far side of the island. I needed sleep but felt movement around my sleeping bag. I shooed away whatever pesky little creature was keeping me awake and then felt a nerve-tingling bite. I screamed in pain from the sting and pulled my hand out of my sleeping bag to find a carpenter ant gripping my right thumb. I ran down the dark path in my pajamas in search of our two counselors, who were having a late-night last hurrah with other counselors before going on the trail, which we campers always imagined was some wild party. Instead, they were just talking over hot cocoa.

I pulled at the ant to loosen its grip but just knocked off its abdomen—its disembodied head kept stinging. The nurse assured me that carpenter ants don't bite, but the evidence proved otherwise. Phil used a needle-nose pliers to yank the ant's head from my thumb. He asked if I still wanted to canoe the next day despite my swollen hand. I said yes—I didn't dare show weakness—and ignored this omen.

After a two-hour van ride into the north woods the next morning, we unloaded our packs from the van and put them into our four canoes on the Totagatic Lake at the river's headwaters. The driver wished us well on this adventure of a lifetime; he would be the last sign of civilization we would see for more than a week. We paddled on the pristine lake under a perfectly sunny sky, but we couldn't find any big river. Instead, we found a small creek, the Totagatic "flowage," which provided some good, disgusting jokes. Apparently, this trickle of water was the legendary Totagatic River.

We walked in the stream holding on to the canoes since it was too shallow and rocky to actually stay aboard—apparently the water level was exceptionally low this year. At times, we had to carry the packs on our backs and portage the canoes over fallen trees and boulders. Only one of the campers could carry a canoe by himself, so Phil and BJ were always portaging the canoes as we lugged the overweight bags. The camp had a "wet boot policy" that required us to never let the boats scrape on rocks, so we always had to jump in the water with our soggy hiking boots.

This went on for three days. The river never opened up, and the rapids on the map were definitely level-IV rapids since they were mostly impassable—because of lack of water. On the fourth day it rained, but our feet had been soaking, or rotting, in water for so long it didn't make a difference. Phil and BJ realized our morale couldn't be lower. If we turned back, wouldn't that be admitting failure? It would be harder to pull the canoes upstream, whereas continuing downstream we at least had the hope of finding open water.

That's when we discovered a hunting shack. No lock closed the door. Obviously the hunters figured that anyone would just rip it off in this remote place. Phil inched open the door, half expecting to find someone inside, but only found a couple of creepy beds and a makeshift little hobo kitchen. We piled into the little cabin and waited out the rain. Phil pulled out the chocolate to raise our spirits. We laughed at the absurdity of our canoe trip with no water.

When the sun came out the next day, we discovered a series of old zip lines from the low cliffs that ran back and forth across the creek. We had no way of knowing if these old wire lines with their rickety pulleys were safe, but how could the counselors deny this fun to these kids who had trudged through mud for four days with packs nearly half their weight. Flying hazardously over the rocky river, we hung on to the pulley handle for dear life, knowing that if our grip slipped, we'd crash into the water, or perhaps on a boulder, fifteen feet below. This danger only made the experience sweeter, even when the wire started to fray. The nearest hospital was days away, and an ambulance, even a helicopter, couldn't reach here.

Then the thought crept into my head that this was probably the Blackburn shack where the notorious ax murder took place nearly a hundred years before. I mentioned this, and some wanted to leave immediately; others wanted to search for lost treasure. It was then that Phil broke the harsh news: the camp van was expecting to pick us up far downstream nine days after it dropped us off. We originally had planned on paddling at least ten miles a day but had managed to portage only two or three. In other words, the van wouldn't have anyone to pick up.

We had to push on, or we might be stuck on this creek for a couple of weeks while a search party scoured the dense woods for us. We hadn't found any gold bullion, but everything was a bit lighter with half of our food eaten and our packs dry again. We tried not to think about what we'd do when we ran out of food. Somehow our spirits were lifted as we went on our hiking trip with canoes on the logging trail that ran parallel to the shallow river. During the next four days, we could occasionally float the canoes for a half hour and even paddle through some areas.

By the morning of the ninth day, we were probably dozens of miles from our pickup site the next day. Fortunately, the creek became a river; we could paddle at last. We were so relieved that we almost didn't notice the car bridge overhead. We hadn't seen any sign of society besides the remote hunting shack and the creaky zip lines. We looked at the overpass as if it was some sort of alien object, all gray and drab amid the lush green forest. Phil yelled for us all to stop. He took the dime taped into the first-aid kit and hitchhiked to a pay phone. By that evening our adventure was over.

On the way back to camp, the van driver stopped at Dairy Queen so Phil could treat us to peanut buster parfaits—ice cream had never tasted so good. The driver admired us for our endurance, though we'd never had a choice but to keep on. Back in camp, we learned that my brother's group had had a perfect time on the Flambeau. But our group was hailed as "heroes" for surviving the trip, as if we hadn't just made a mistake and then paid for it. I joked that if you want to "build character," just sleep in a swamp for a week and somehow you're a better person. Phil felt terrible for leading us on a trip on the Totagatic, which we later learned translates from Ojibwe as "place of floating bogs." Strangely, we were sad that our canoe trip on a nonexistent river was over.

NO ROAD TO CAMP

THE YEAR AFTER MY CANOE TRIP IN WISCONSIN, I TOLD MY parents I was done with camp. They understood my hesitation but pointed out that last summer's hike with canoes was a fluke. "Which camp do you want to try now?" my mom asked as she showed me brochures showing kids climbing trees, sailing, and laughing hysterically. I remembered that I loved swimming in the freshwater and all the games at camp. I convinced myself that canoeing across wide-open lakes would be far simpler than portaging down a creek, even if I still couldn't carry a canoe alone. My parents signed me up for a wilderness camp on the southern edge of the Boundary Waters Canoe Area that could be accessed only by boat.

Even after vowing to stay away from any camp after the previous summer, I found myself on a rickety yellow school bus bouncing around on rutted roads toward the Canadian border. The road simply dead-ended at a lake, and the bus skidded to a stop. A thirty-foot voyageur canoe filled with counselors pulled up on the shore to pick us up.

Tim, a well-tanned veteran camper topped with a Campagnolo Italian cycling cap, hopped off the boat with the counselors and introduced himself; he'd been a counselor-in-training for the previous two weeks and would show me how things were done here.

He helped me load my pack onto the big boat, and we discovered we'd be in the same cabin group. We grabbed paddles to help row the giant fiberglass canoe across West Bearskin Lake to the remote wilderness camp. No cabins were visible anywhere on the lake. Tim explained that no motorized boats are allowed in the Boundary Waters, so we had to rely on our own wits to survive.

From the water, we could finally see the little boathouse and dock that extended out to greet us. I'd been here once before. My parents had brought me here in the dead of winter, so we had skied across the frozen lake to reach the camp. At the time, everyone was gathered in the sauna, or "Finn bath," as some called it, which they stoked to nearly 190 degrees. We stripped down to sweat inside, but I remember being shocked at what followed. Our host told us, "Now you either roll in the snow or jump into the hole in the lake. If you don't, your sweat will just freeze on you, and you'll never be clean." I didn't dare doubt this questionable advice, so I rolled in the snow the first time, which was rough and granular. The next time I risked cardiac arrest and jumped into the large hole cut in the ice. I couldn't breathe in the glacial water and exited so fast I barely got wet.

Now during the summer, the sauna was reserved for those about to leave on the trail—the last bath for at least ten days—or those just returning. Tim told us that the counselors wanted to make sure the kids didn't stink too much before being sent home. Because he thought we already smelled, our twenty-year-old counselor, Dave, reserved the sauna that evening for our group of eight campers, all around fourteen years old. Adam and Keith bonded right away since their parents forced them to go to camp. Adam said his dad wanted to toughen him because he only wanted to read *Robin Hood* and other classics rather than being outside; Keith said his mom did not want him to waste his life away in the basement playing video games and listening to Black Sabbath. He wanted to show his mother that he wasn't going to enjoy camp. Somehow little John, who was only thirteen but looked ten, annoyed everyone by trying to show he was the toughest—lifting more than he should, breaking branches against trees, and cussing whenever he opened his mouth. Tim tried to remain above any bickering and thought he was the natural leader, despite being just a camper-in-training. John mocked Keith, who complained bitterly about the painful heat of the sauna. Adam viewed it as an adventure, a test out of the *Arabian Nights,* and Dave just told everyone to be quiet and enjoy the luxury of the moment.

"Luxury? Sweating in this dirty wooden shack?" Keith scoffed.

This wilderness camp had not changed much since being founded in the 1920s, except for the addition of electricity to the dining hall. Dave and Tim considered austerity an advantage, Keith was horrified, and the rest of us needed to be convinced.

After the sauna, the only light to guide us to our sleeping bags was a kerosene lantern and flashlight beams, moving haphazardly like mini searchlights. Tim led us to the outhouse before bed and told John that he had to pull the cord dangling down inside the outhouse to flush it when he was done. The rope was attached to a bell outside the outhouse to announce to all that a newcomer had arrived. Surprisingly, John didn't swear but laughed and in turn played the trick on Keith, who was not amused.

That night in our sleeping bags, Dave told everyone to be quiet and go to sleep. Instead Tim told us tales of grueling six-week trips other groups from the camp had taken into Canada's Northwest Territories. They ended their trip a few days early at Hudson Bay and waited to be picked up by the floatplane, but a curious polar bear discovered them first. They barricaded themselves into a little whaling shack along the shore but soon remembered that polar bears are the only animals besides humans who hunt for sport. The bear ripped apart the door and barged into the cabin just as they rushed out the window and onto the roof. Tim said he saw photos taken from the roof of the snorting nose and paws of the giant bear peering over the eaves. They had hoped the flash would scare off the beast. The bear would leave for a while and then return to torment them. A couple of beluga whale hunters saved them by scaring off the beast by shooting into the air. They gave the campers some flares to shoot if the bear came back. Obviously the campers were ready to leave when their floatplane arrived to take them home. Tim said that despite nearly being mauled by polar bears, the group raved about the experience and couldn't wait to go back. Tim advised us that these difficult experiences are the most rewarding because then you realize you can overcome anything.

We didn't need to worry about polar bears eating us alive since our trip would be a simple ten-day jaunt through the Boundary Waters. The next morning when we loaded our packs into the canoes, they rode low in the water. Dave had packed lots of salami, chocolate, and cheese since he had planned a remote route that had lots of portages. "We're getting away from everything," Dave remarked.

"And why would we want to do that?" Keith asked, but Adam answered for the counselor that this was an adventure, an odyssey into the unknown. Keith wasn't convinced.

Our extra food rations gave us much needed energy, and the food pack quickly got lighter. Our fourth day on the trip, we took a layover day with no travel to relax. We jumped off low cliffs into the refreshing water below, and Dave made a feast of some sort of lentil-rice mixture that is only delicious when on the trail. Tim advised us to save up energy for the last several days before we arrived back at camp for a well-deserved sauna.

Perhaps we were too refreshed and rested; we became careless. While portaging, Tim, the only kid who could portage a canoe by himself, hyperextended his knee. The awkward weight of the canoe forced his knee to bend backwards when he stepped on a rock. He was able to stumble over the portages between lakes, despite the discomfort, but couldn't carry anything else. Suddenly, we had to take two trips over portages and get Tim back to civilization as early as possible. The push was on.

Dave was clearly flustered by the fact that there was no way to get Tim out except for paddling with eight kids. He tried to stay calm, but I continually asked, "Do you know where we are?" because he clearly didn't. We had no GPS, so Dave consulted the compass and map but often missed the small, hidden portages at the ends of the lakes and had to backtrack. We judged the direction by the sun or looked for moss growing mostly on the north side of trees. We learned how to roughly judge how many hours until sunset by extending an arm and putting our palm toward us to measure about one hour per hand width.

With our food sack more than half depleted, we doubled up on carrying bags, and I managed to carry a canoe with Keith. Exhausted by late afternoon, he yelped in pain when we set down the canoe. He said that he had dislocated his shoulder. Dave ran to help him, but Keith wouldn't let anyone touch his throbbing arm, which dangled at his side. Instead, Keith used his T-shirt for a makeshift sling.

Dave debated what to do. He could paddle a canoe alone for a day to a resort on the edge of the Boundary Waters, find a phone, and call in a floatplane to fly the injured campers out at a cost of thousands of dollars. Now Dave's dream of being in the middle of nowhere haunted him.

"Maybe we should cut off Tim's leg," John wondered matter-of-factly.

"Then he'd have a peg leg like a pirate!" Adam added.

"Um, excuse me, I'm still here," Tim reminded them.

"It's kind of like Robinson Crusoe," said Adam. "We can't travel with two cripples, so we just need to set up our colony here on an island and hope to be rescued."

"Isn't it supposed to be like 'survival of the fittest' in the wilderness?" John said. "In that case, shouldn't we just leave them or eat them or something?"

Nobody responded to John's ludicrous ideas, but I seriously pondered making a run for it in one of the canoes. Dave told everyone to calm down. We all agreed to sleep just a few hours that night, and then be up way before dawn to canoe all day to get them to the lodge where a car could fetch them. We could rest tomorrow afternoon.

The gravity of the situation gave us energy to wake up at four. The strongest campers, Tim and Keith, could no longer carry anything, so we stumbled over the portages with canoes and packs through ankle-deep mud. Fortunately, the early morning moon was nearly full, so the lake was brightly lit. We relied on the North Star for direction.

I have never seen a more welcome sight than the sun peeking over the treetops, lighting our way. A breeze kicked up to whisk away the mosquitoes, feeding on our luscious, oxygenated blood. Waves with white caps slowed us down across the large stretches of lakes, conditions that normally would leave wise expeditions wind bound for the day. Adam kept up a steady monologue about our adventure, comparing it to every expedition he'd read about. "Ol' Mother Nature can be cruel!" he chirped happily to keep up our spirits.

"Oh shut up! Won't you please just be quiet?" Dave snapped.

We had hoped to arrive at the lodge by midafternoon after paddling twelve hours, but Dave told us we still had two more lakes to cross. No one said a word at this point; we just trudged on, wishing that Adam would be our announcer. When the rain came, I just laughed. At this point, I knew that nothing could stop us. Perhaps recognizing our determination, the showers gave up after an hour, and the sun warmed our backs.

We continued paddling as the sun set in the distance—why weren't we there yet? I didn't dare ask Dave.

At ten o'clock we saw the distant yellow glow of the lodge across the lake—the first electric lights we'd seen in seven days. The vacationers lounging on the dock were shocked to see this ragtag group of wet canoers pull up to the shore. Dave told us to wait in the canoes as he brought Tim and Keith inside.

"What? Don't we get to go to the restaurant for dinner?" John asked, the first sign of mutiny I'd heard. Dave returned to tell us that the restaurant was closed, and besides, they didn't have money for all of us to eat. Instead, he brought us chocolate bars, which were the most exquisite treat imaginable at the time.

Tim and Keith returned to say good-bye since they would be staying at the lodge for the night until someone from the camp picked them up the next day. Keith then announced that his shoulder didn't hurt so much, and perhaps it was just sprained. "Yeah, when we were traveling today, it felt much better. I didn't want to get anyone upset, though, so I just kept it to myself." We all wanted to strangle him since he hadn't carried a thing, but obviously he'd gotten his wish—his mother wouldn't be sending him back next year.

Somehow, we thought that we were staying there too, but we were too tired to talk back when Dave said we could take two days of doing nothing at our campsite before we went back to camp. Nothing could faze us by then; we knew we could accomplish anything. Our mission was accomplished, so my life as a camper was complete. Like the living dead, we paddled down the shore in search of a campsite. We had won our battle, but nothing mattered anymore except for sleeping for two days. The cool wind pitied us and blew all the bugs away as we slept under the stars that had guided us.

ANOTHER DAY AT AMERICAN CAMP

I HAD NO PLANS TO BECOME A CAMP COUNSELOR. NONE. I HAD been backpacking around Italy, when I ran out of money and couches to sleep on. My French friend, François, recruited me to an experimental American camp in the south of France. I asked whether it was a good idea having eighteen- to twenty-year-olds in charge of kids in a foreign country. He knew my French was laughable, but I could smile and nod like a pro and employ "ooh-la-la"–type expressions with native-like timing. He assured me I was perfect for the job and reminded me that I was twenty-three now and obviously responsible enough to travel around Europe. Only later did I find out that they were hard up for counselors.

A little yellow train brought me up to the highest railway station in France and left me at Font Romeu right along the Spanish border in the Pyrenees. The dean, her husband, and François were helping the caretakers do away with large quantities of local wine before the kids arrived. They poured me a glass. I realized this wasn't a typical U.S. work environment. But we had to make the camp resemble the United States despite the surroundings, which included a stone fourteenth-century monastery called "L'Ermitage," which roughly means "hermit's house"—probably the furthest from a typical American town we could get.

To be certified, we all had to submit to four days of lectures by an administrator from the official French camping agency, Nacel, all in nearly impossible-to-follow Gallic bureaucratic lingo. After some good naps during the meetings, we were well rested for the arrival of the kids. One by one *les enfants* filed off the bus from Paris. Aged eight to twelve, these French children would be immersed in American culture and English language for two weeks. They lined up to choose a new name and identity, and no one wanted the stereotypical monosyllabic American names like Bob, Bill, Jane, or Jill. Instead, our sophisticated four-foot-high campers opted for such dignified and dated titles as Sylvester, Arnold, Booker, Thelma, Edna, Thelonious, and Bartholomew.

As the song-leading counselor, I led English lessons each day. Rather than filling out worksheets, we played games, and I strummed a guitar for sing-alongs. "Yankee Doodle" was deemed too square, and *les enfants terribles* wanted the punk rock Social Distortion song "Ball and Chain." I realized my lesson plan on family relations needed some work when I asked Alexander, "Who is the husband of his aunt?"

"Goldfish," he replied confidently. He then looked at my Minnesota Twins cap and asked if he could try on my "baseball crap."

Most of the French kids immediately recognized these sessions as "work," which was in direct conflict with their God-given right to have summers off.

"*Je rêve!*" (I'm dreaming!), little Gertrude slapped her forehead with her palm in disbelief. "*Ce n'est pas possible!*" (It's not possible!).

Kendall, a cute kid with his finger constantly in his nose, tried to calm her down, but Gertrude argued that you never tell a French woman to calm down (she was ten). "*C'est dégueulasse!*" (This is disgusting!), she exclaimed and crossed her arms in protest.

Her best friend Evelyn held up her left fist in solidarity and exclaimed, "*J'en ai marre et je m'en fous!*" (I'm fed up and I don't give a damn!).

Arnold came back from the bathroom—he always had to go as soon as we had some work to do—and asked, "*Qu'est-ce que c'est que ce bordel?*" (What is this whorehouse?). When Evelyn and Gertrude explained that I was a slave driver forcing them to learn English, Arnold swore, "*C'est chiant!*" (This is a pain in the ass!).

I started writing down their objections so I could learn these new ways to express dissatisfaction in French. They assumed I was mocking them, and perhaps I was. Only when they declared a general strike and marched around the table chanting, "*On fait la grève!*" (We're going on strike!) did I call for backup.

In spite of their perky rebellious nature, the campers proved to be typical kids with the usual quirks and constant cuts, scrapes, and bruises. One camper, Reginald, showed that he could clear the whole dining hall after eating green beans if he wasn't given his daily dose of flatulence medicine. Kendall recovered from his compulsive nose picking when he tripped while running between first and second base playing baseball. His finger was digging away in his nostril, and he didn't remove it even to break his fall. "I just can't keep my finger out of there!" he confessed. In spite of the bruised elbow, his parents thanked us later for curing this bad habit.

We learned good judgment by trial and error. Mark, a counselor from South Carolina who would dress up as a middle-aged French woman with a squeaky voice to make the kids laugh, challenged his cabin to see who could drink the most milk. When the remnants of the contest manifested themselves later that evening, he decided that a water-drinking contest would be much healthier.

François entrusted me and another counselor to take a group of kids hiking up in the mountains for an overnight camping trip. He dropped us off in the van and said that about two miles up the path was an open cabin for trekkers. With no map and no phone, we ventured through the spider web of paths in search of the small cabin that François had assured us was there. Finally at about sundown, we found the small cottage, which was filled with mice nibbling on morsels of leftover camembert. So instead, we slept out in a field with no tent. Not one insect bothered us, and the stars lit up the sky as though we'd punctured a million holes in a roof that couldn't keep out the brilliance. We were lost in the mountains, but somehow it didn't matter—the Milky Way made it all OK.

The next morning, François easily found us and brought us back to L'Ermitage for lunch, which was *soupe, salade,* and *steak* with a bottle of ketchup on the table to make it seem American. We found that the other kids had taken over the stone courtyard in the center of the monastery as a soccer field. Pilgrims still stopped to sip the curative waters of the enclosed fountain at the wall of the church. The entrance to the fountain doubled as a goal for one of the soccer teams, so the game abruptly ended when one of the faithful pilgrims unwittingly saved the ball from scoring with her head while bending to pray.

The priest yelled at me and another counselor (in spicy French) about endangering the lives of his parishioners, and the campers had to translate this tirade into their often indecipherable English. Mark and I had to explain to the campers that beaning pilgrims in the head was bad for church business, especially when they were bowing to the Almighty. In true camp spirit, we added that the mysterious "hermit" of the Ermitage could come out from his hole and grab the naughty campers—especially the identical twins Seymour and Sylvester who streaked naked through the bedrooms every night. Within the hour, rumors had spread that somewhere in the monastery lived the ghost of an evil hermit.

To get the campers' minds off the hermit, we arranged a *"boom,"* or dance, the last night. The campers had packed formal clothes for the occasion and spent the evening primping for the ball. Hair was greased back, and showers of cologne were squirted on any exposed skin. The favorite songs—apart from those of Social Distortion—involved lots of gestures: the Chicken Dance, the Bunny Hop, the Hokey Pokey. Suddenly any music was OK because we were having a party. When a slow song oozed out of the speakers, the boys and girls, who hid secret crushes, forgot their usual Tarzan etiquette and asked their darlings for a dance. Suddenly these preteens seemed years older, though the average relationship barely lasted through the three-minute song.

Some of the campers were already bored with the dance and, tugging at my arm, asked me to help them find the hermit at the fountain. Mark and I cursed ourselves for inventing the story but decided to take the bravest campers into this holy room. We brought candles to the dark and musty entrance to the trickling fountain. The gate creaked open to reveal moss-covered walls lined with crutches left by pilgrims cured by the holy water. As we sat around the fountain waiting for the hermit, Bartholomew nervously told the ghost story of the Dame Blanche who sleeps in the street. "If you stare out long enough at the road in the dark, you'll see her!" The campers challenged each other to hold up their index fingers, shut their eyes, and let the spirit of the hermit enter their bodies. Worried that they'd be led like a pilgrim down into the circles of hell, no one dared do it. In the flickering light of the candles reflecting off the water of the fountain, I could see the campers shivering with fear and fascination.

Suddenly the door was flung open, and the wind blew out the candle. The campers screamed as another counselor yelled to me, "Eric! Quick, quick! You've got to come save Seymour!" The mock séance was being interrupted by Seymour threatening to throw himself out a second-story window. I found Seymour, one of the identical twins who had been happily running around naked earlier, precariously standing on the window ledge with tears streaming down his face. Kendall, the ex–nose picker, was singing "Yankee Doodle Dandy" to him to try to calm him down. Seymour bawled that his beloved Beatrice didn't want to dance with him and liked Arnold instead. Seymour had heard that she even kissed him in the courtyard. My heart was racing as I thought about how to diffuse this situation and avoid a flattened camper. I thought maybe I could grab him from the window, but I feared that would only force him to jump or else we'd both tumble down two stories into the stone courtyard. Instead, I told him in my rough French that I had heard Gertrude and Evelyn had a crush on him. He cried that he could love only Beatrice. She was his true love, and only she could make him happy.

I envisioned calling Seymour's parents to explain that their lovestruck eight-year-old had taken a lover's leap. Then I suggested we sip some hot chocolate in the cafeteria and talk about it.

"*Chocolat chaud? Maintenant?*" he wept and wiped away his tears. He hopped off the windowsill as if nothing had happened and ran to get his hot cocoa.

The shaking survivors from the holy fountain joined us in the dining hall for *le cinquième,* or fifth meal, a camp tradition in France possible thanks to the long days of summer. We didn't feel like celebrating to the Hokey Pokey back at the *boom.* Instead, we let the warm chocolate elixir soothe our insides, and we pondered how we had beaten the grim reaper—or the hermit.

ME? A DEAN?

"You want me to run an Italian summer camp? Me?" I replied, shocked that someone had nominated me for the position. "What do I know about running a camp?"

I was a graduate teaching assistant at the University of Minnesota in the Italian department and had just found out that a friend who runs a Swedish language camp thought that I'd be a good choice to run the Italian camp. I'd heard of these immersion camps that re-create their respective countries or language groups in northern Minnesota. Fifteen different languages are taught at different beachside campsites nestled in the woods. Then I learned that the Italian camp was the small cousin to the large German and French camps. The administrators had decided not to rehire the past Italian dean, and I soon realized they wanted someone from the outside to stop the infighting.

Since I didn't have a summer job, I applied for the position, assuming that the camp administrators would likely find someone else, such as a fully qualified Ph.D. or at least an elementary teacher who knew the pedagogy. My wife, Katy, and I reasoned that the advantage of working at the camp would be that our two boys could attend for free when they grew up. The dean of the camp in France warned me, "Do you want to live intensely? If so, do it. Otherwise relax and say 'no.'"

Somehow, I passed the first round of candidate interviews, and I can only guess that they assumed my last name, "Dregni," must be Italian, despite its Norwegian origin as "Drægni." Following an awkward conference call interview with several other camp directors, including my French friend François, the organization offered me the position. Soon, I was flooded with three-ring binders full of all the crucial information needed to run a camp. As I waded through the material, I found that not only did I have to set the daily schedule, activities, and curriculum, but I also had to hire the staff. Realizing this was a massive amount of work while I was still studying Dante for my master's degree, I tried to quit. Twice. I left the administrators with months to find someone else, but they wouldn't accept my resignation.

I had very few applications from previous staff—apparently many of them had vowed never to return. Almost none of the new candidates who applied were qualified. I essentially needed counselors who

- didn't object to kids hanging on them all day and then sleeping in the same cabin with them,

- were free to work half of the summer for very little money,

- liked to live outdoors (with spiders, snakes, and stinging nettle),

- didn't mind having almost no privacy (especially in the cabin and in the showers),

- thought electricity and clean clothes were unnecessary luxuries,

- were inspired to wear ridiculous outfits for goofy skits,

- could lead sing-alongs in front of more than fifty people,

- preferably played guitar and were lifeguards,
- and—this is the catch—were fluent in Italian.

Obviously, these qualifications limited the pool of applicants. Even those potential counselors who met these qualifications had very . . . well . . . pronounced personalities. Many had specific food issues (gluten-free, egg-free, walnut-free, onion-free, pesco-ovo, vegans . . .), which were usually navigable, but one potential counselor announced, "I only eat local, organic food; I'm a locavore." While I said this was admirable, I told her that I doubted if the kitchen staff could source all of their ingredients to within fifty miles, and if they did, we'd be eating mostly beets and corn. She told me that this would be all right, but I worried that she'd forage in the forest or have her own bizarre food stash.

During a phone interview with another promising applicant, she exposed the extent of her love of nature. "My best friends are 'treants,'" she confessed.

"You mean those living trees that are alive, like those ones in *Wizard of Oz*?" I wondered.

"Yes, or in *Dungeons and Dragons*. Most people think they don't exist, but I do," she clarified, apparently having forgotten this was a job interview. Although I'd have loved to watch what might unfold in the woods, I realized I wouldn't want her as a counselor for my own kids.

I understand we all have quirks, but I was worried I wouldn't find out about them until we had sixty campers in our care. I resolved to surreptitiously scope out other students at the University of Minnesota who studied Italian. I made a list and began crossing them out one by one.

First was Katia, an outgoing sorority girl, who had returned from a semester in Florence. I constantly pushed the university students to spend a year in Italy and expounded on all the wonderful art and architecture, but they didn't hear me. Katia stood in front of the class and exclaimed, "Guys, you gotta go! It's the best." With no description or any details, Katia got them to sign up.

After class, she asked me to examine her Italian composition for another class since she was scared of "Zeus, that crazy bearded professor who just looks at me funny." We sat outside on a bench under oak trees where gray squirrels were frolicking from branch to branch. As I pointed out how to improve her writing, she jumped suddenly and scanned around us nervously.

"Is everything OK?" I asked.

"I'm terrified of squirrels," she admitted. "Look! There's an albino one! Oh my God, this is like my worst nightmare." Obviously she would not do well in the woods.

Another potential candidate from France who spoke Italian ranted about how Americans were crazy because of how much we work. "Work to live, not live to work!" he advised me. Although he might be right, I didn't want to be his manager.

An important attribute of a camp counselor is being able to adapt to different situations. Some native Italians at the university were horrified by how we live and shocked we didn't have bars on all our windows. "What's to stop thieves from just walking right in?" Another Italian asked me, "Why are your houses made of wood. Isn't that dangerous? In Italy they'd all burn down since we always smoke cigarettes." Considering the houses at camp are log cabins, their paranoia could be problematic and worry the kids.

Another teaching assistant, Marie, jumped in to the conversation, telling me, "You Americans are pigs!" I'd heard this before, especially after Europeans saw that students didn't wash their dishes right after eating. Marie handed us a flyer for a contest for the "dirtiest apartment award" showing the utter filth of the living conditions. "How can you live like this? You don't sit down while you eat. You drink coffee while walking. What's the matter with you?"

I stuck up for Americans by rebutting, "We're really not so bad, and that contest is a fluke." Just then we both saw an American teaching assistant walking down a flight of steps, forking tuna fish into his mouth from a can. I conceded, "OK, you win . . ." Although she might have been right, I didn't think she'd fit in among dirty little kids.

I pointed out that I didn't eat like that, and opened my lunch sack with an apple, some carrots, and a tomato and cheese on rye. An American student stared longingly, "Oh, you have a sandwich; that looks great. I wish I had a sandwich."

Perhaps it was my duty to feed them. Besides, hosting a big meal could be a good test to see if any of my students would make good counselors. One of my students, Johnny, was a chef at an upscale Italian restaurant and would cook as long as everyone chipped in ten dollars for the shopping; my wife, Katy, and I would do the prep work.

With his hefty list in hand, I scoured the aisles of the grocery store and carried the requested Italian ingredients to the checkout. The stocky cashier had never seen many of these vegetables and asked her colleague at the next register for help with the names— artichokes, capers, sun-dried tomatoes, basil—so she could check her price list. She examined a bulb of fennel, which is sometimes called anise.

The other cashier replied, "It's called 'anus.'"

"Thanks!" she replied and announced into her microphone,

blaring throughout the store, "OK, price check on register four! This guy's got a big bunch of anus here." The disturbed shoppers waiting in line scowled at me.

Katy and I spent the day mincing and dicing the produce so the chef/student could come in and make a disaster of our kitchen. Rather than using a can opener, he plunged a large kitchen knife into the top of a tin of tomatoes. "It's just faster," he explained as he cleared the counter of unused ingredients by flicking them to the floor. As in the restaurant, he expected the sous-chef to sweep up his mess.

In spite of the kitchen catastrophe, the meal was perfect. The twelve students exclaimed that they'd never seen such a spread: antipasto of bruschetta; a pasta course of linguine with sun-dried tomato sauce; three main courses of grilled swordfish topped with lemon pesto, halibut smothered in caramelized balsamic vinegar, and chicken with a creamy truffle sauce; side dishes of sautéed carrots and green beans with garlic potatoes; and two desserts of *tiramisù* and amaretto drizzled on *gelato alla vaniglia* over flourless chocolate torte.

I was observing the students to see who would make a good counselor, but they were all being reserved at the dinner, probably because as their instructor, I would be giving them a grade at the end of the semester. I posed the question, would they be interested in working at an Italian camp this summer? Chad, a friendly frat boy who plays football, declared that he was a Food Channel junky. He cooked for the rest of his fraternity but only had a microwave and only cooked blood sausage. "Chasing kids around all summer? I don't think that's my thing," he declared.

A shy African American student from Palo Alto cryptically said that he speaks "Ebonics," which is why I could rarely understand him. He'd never been in the forest and was more interested in teaching English in Milan. "If I do that, will they know that I can't speak English?" I told him that he'd probably be very popular because of his slang, noting that none of the Italian students I had taught in Italy had wanted to learn the "Queen's English."

A diligent music student from small-town Minnesota seemed a likely candidate since he could lead sing-alongs with the kids. The rest of the students pushed him to perform for us at the dinner. Rather than playing the piano or strumming my guitar for accompaniment, he belted out an out-of-tune opera aria with a shaky voice. He stared us in the eyes to show his sincerity during the a cappella warbling, as we all looked down, embarrassed and praying for a quick ending. After the excruciating cacophony, we politely clapped as he nearly broke down in tears with joy from the applause.

The last option for a counselor was a quiet Wisconsinite from Madison who listened to Marvin Gaye through his earbuds and attended all the University of Minnesota hockey games. He had phoned to say that he would drop off his final composition but couldn't stay for the dinner. He showed up with a black eye, his arm in a cast, and a big smile on his face. After he left, I skimmed through his essay in Italian about how he had gotten drunk with friends the previous evening before the championship hockey game. To celebrate the victory, students had pulled down streetlights, started a bonfire on University Avenue, and overturned parked cars. The Minneapolis police had beat him up and thrown him in jail for inciting a riot. He loved it.

Despite the delicious dinner and a mess of a kitchen, my quest to find worthy counselors in my class was a flop. I realized I'd have to look elsewhere.

BEAVER PRIDE

How could I find Italian-speaking counselors to work for very little money in northern Minnesota? I called up all the staff from the previous summer to see if they'd come back to camp, and one of them, Lucrezia, said, "Maybe. Just maybe." As long as a new dean was taking over, they would consider returning. What sort of hornet's nest was I stirring up? I dreaded we would have divisions between the old and new staff, between the native Italians and the Americans, and perhaps between the male and female counselors.

Katy and I invited several of the American staff from the previous year to dinner to convince them to return and perhaps be my allies. I immediately mixed up Lucrezia and Letizia, who had both been at Italian camp every year of its existence but looked nothing alike. "It's OK, everyone confuses us," Lucrezia assured me.

I introduced myself as "Eric."

"No," Letizia warned me sternly. "You can't use the name 'Eric' at camp. You need an Italian name." I didn't think we were off to such a good start. I happen to be rather attached to my name, even if Italians generally add an *H* to the beginning of my name to pronounce it "headache."

I thought a minute and said, "My brother nicknamed me 'Dario.'"

I explained that he came up with the name because I zoomed around full speed on my Lambretta motor scooter just like Dario Ambrosini, the Moto Benelli works racer who would test drive and compete on these Italian motorcycles.

"What happened to him?" Lucrezia asked.

"Well . . ." I hesitated. "He crashed into a telephone pole and died." They seemed worried, so I quickly changed the subject and confessed that perhaps this was why I needed their expertise to make the Italian camp function.

"What? So we don't crash into a telephone pole?" Lucrezia asked.

Martina, who was proud of her rowdy Wisconsin upbringing, arrived and eased the tension with her enthusiasm. She carried on the conversation for all of us, throwing in just enough gossip to keep us interested but not too much to be scandalous. She even gave me a backhanded compliment, "Dario, no matter what you do, you can't be any worse than the last dean." She divulged that last year's counselors listed all of the old dean's shortcomings including how confrontational she was. Martina asked if I wanted to see it.

"Umm, no, I really don't," I squirmed, worried that they were already preparing a list about me. Perhaps they were wondering if I was on the old dean's side, even though I'd never met her.

"What you need is for Zeta to come back as assistant dean," Letizia advised.

"Yeah, Zeta's from Milwaukee, so she's great," Martina added cryptically.

"Every year she swears she'll never come back," Letizia said, "but you just have to convince her that we desperately need her or the camp will fall apart."

"This is just a game she plays," Lucrezia assured me. "She refuses to come to orientation, but that doesn't matter. She doesn't say much, but she knows everything."

I'd already struck out trying to hire my students to be counselors, so I waded through the applications for new American staff. They might look great on paper but were sometimes baffling in interviews, and I worried they might be completely different around the kids. The application of a college student from Boston didn't stand out, but on the phone she oozed enthusiasm when she exclaimed, "I love camp!" She was perfect counselor material and chose the name "Tiziana," which some of the administrators mispronounced "Dizzy-ana" with a soft *z* sound. She corrected them, telling them that the pronunciation was "TITS-ee-ana," and she liked to watch them squirm. Later at camp, she asked, "Where's my shirt?" and unabashedly wore a bright American flag bikini instead. My guess was she'd be popular with the Italian male staff.

Once I hired the staff, I reached out to them in hopes they'd view me less as a boss and more as a friend and confidant. When Sergio arrived in Minneapolis directly from the Alps of Piedmont, I picked him up at the airport. This mountain man stood more than six feet tall and was topped with a leather cowboy hat. He was muscular but clean shaven with perfectly pressed clothes. His brightly colored Hawaiian shirt—he thought this was a typical American outfit—was muted only by a khaki vest with pockets filled with gadgets, mosquito repellant, a compass, and other necessities to take on the northern wilderness.

He greeted me warmly and folded his long legs into my tiny Honda Civic for the five-hour drive north to Bemidji for our week-long staff orientation. He swore and blasphemed smoothly in his thick northern accent while telling me that he was pleased that last month he had been officially thrown out of the Catholic Church for writing several letters to his local newspaper questioning the church's policies. "I have an official letter from the Vatican excommunicating me!" he said proudly. I admitted I was rather impressed, if concerned.

As we drove, I learned that he had chosen the name "Sergio" for camp rather than retaining his real name because his idol was Sergio Leone, the great spaghetti Western director. "This is my dream to come to America to see the real West," he told me. I didn't tell him that those films were shot mostly in Spain and Italy or that Minnesota is definitely not Dodge City.

I treated him to root beer, and he was thrilled with this exotic beverage that the cowboys drank. He bought a case of it to mail back to Italy. At the post office, though, he discovered that the six dollars' worth of soda cans would cost him nearly fifty dollars to ship home. "Instead, I must drink as much root beer as possible while I'm in Minnesota."

To cheer him up, I looked for other places to show him during our drive. "I hear in America you can buy guns at shopping malls. Is this true?" he asked. "I am licensed to have a gun back home." I considered bringing him to a wilderness outfitter to see the disturbing assortment of high-caliber firearms, but I didn't want an armed Italian at camp.

Instead, we stopped at a western saddle shop that had a hokey wood fence, supposedly to tie up your horses next to the acre of parked SUVs. Inside, Sergio blissfully tried on cowboy shirts with rhinestone buttons and lapels embroidered with little horsey patterns.

He coveted a gaudy belt buckle with the Confederate flag, and I shook my head in disapproval. He judged it as a bit of Americana kitsch, but I explained that it would be like me wearing a T-shirt of

Mussolini conquering Somalia. Fortunately, he was distracted by the turquoise bolo ties with silver horse-shoe designs.

The shopkeeper wore beat-up Wrangler jeans, broken-in boots, and a well-used straw hat. His calm western accent floated gently next to Sergio's barrage of Italian blaspheming. This was a real Oklahoma cowboy who was up north to shoe horses and worked in the shop on Saturdays.

Sergio caressed a pair of red-and-white cowboy boots and dreamed of a real ten-gallon Stetson hat. He put his stack of new clothes next to the register, all ready to check out. He showed off his new cowboy clothes, which outshone even his Hawaiian shirt.

"Whoa! Those are some fancy duds," the cowboy asked. "Are you going to a party? You must be gettin' gussied up for a hoedown."

"No, I am from Italy," Sergio responded, as if this was an explanation.

"That's grand. So you're here to ride horses, eh?" asked the Okie.

"Actually, I have never been on a horse," Sergio replied, unaware of the irony. "I do like to eat them, though."

The cowboy laughed, assuming this must be a joke, and politely rang up the more than two-hundred-dollar tab of silver bolo ties and other gaudy cowboy knickknacks that the Oklahoman would never wear.

Another northern Italian, Paola from Brescia, had her first glimpse of the United States in Bemidji, Minnesota, where we were to have our weeklong orientation. "Ah, this is America!" she exclaimed when she saw the giant statue of Paul Bunyan and Babe the Blue Ox.

"I suppose . . ." I hesitated, "but there's a bit more to America. You know: New York, Chicago, California . . ."

"Yes, of course, but for me this is all I see, so this is America for me!" I understood her point, but following this logic, she might believe that towns from coast to coast have oversized statues of lumberjacks in plaid flannel and off-colored cows.

I realized the American staff had our work cut out for us to familiarize the Italians with northern Minnesota. Irene from Turin practiced her broken English by reading all the road signs along the way. She saw a motel along remote Highway 2 with a neon sign of evergreens that read "Whispering Pines." She told her American cousin Gabriella, "Oh we've arrived at Whispering Penis!"

The American staff from the East Coast were shocked that Bemidji State University proudly abbreviates its name as BSU. The Italians wanted to know the joke, so I explained that BS can mean "bullshit."

"But BS means 'Brescia'!" Paola added.

"Now we know what your town really is!" responded Simone from Civitavecchia.

"The university must call BS for the blue bull of which they are so proud," Irene pointed out.

To make matters worse, the Americans laughed in disbelief when they found out the BSU mascot is the "beaver." I reluctantly explained to the Italians that this word can refer to women's privates.

"I think this is beautiful that they honor women here," said Paola, pointing to the giant "Beaver Pride" banners. "Why not? Why be embarrassed?"

I imagined these intentional double meanings made the new Italians believe that it was more liberal here than in Italy. Tiziana told me she entered the staff room and noticed Sergio on the couch alone. "Do you want to make out?" he asked her nonchalantly, and Tiziana quickly made for the exit. Another Italian told me, "You

Americans are stuck in the sixties. In America, you smoke marijuana, but in Italy young people like Ecstasy," though he assured me that none of this would happen at camp.

While this openness might have been refreshing, I had to be the party pooper. I led a session to inform the staff that once at camp I was required to terminate their employment if they drank or did anything illegal. The new staff looked at me, fearful that I would send them home. Martina nodded, happy that I'd laid down the law. To lighten the mood, we watched the cult camp film *Wet Hot American Summer* and counted all the ways they could be fired.

Most of the Italians arrived with slick new clothes (completely unprepared for the north woods) in bulky but beautiful suitcases. The American staff generally had a rucksack, and Bonifacio, from Cameroon, arrived with his duffel bag and a nice green, five-gallon pail. Katy asked him why he brought a bucket, and Bonifacio responded, "I never know where I'll be staying, so I can use it to wash my clothes and many other things." The bucket kept his clothes dry if there was a puddle, unlike his bag, and it could double as a stool.

Katy told me, "After he explained why he brings his bucket around, I thought that maybe I should do it too."

The airline lost the suitcase of Michele from Basilicata. He arrived at ten in the evening, five hours north of Minneapolis, with only the clothes on his back. The airline promised to drive his bag all the way up in a few days. "Look at me, I'm a mess!" he proclaimed while sweating in the ninety-five degree heat.

He looked at the American staff dressed so casually and deduced that anything goes here. He insisted on going to Walmart late at night when he heard that it never closes. "That is perverse," he exclaimed gleefully, "and so American!" He returned dressed in a polyester XXXL T-shirt—more than two sizes too large for him—with a pattern of thousands of juicy hamburgers dripping with ketchup—or was it blood? Thrilled with his new shirt, he proclaimed, "I love the American hamburger."

Nina from Torino, on the other hand, was thin and tastefully dressed. She rolled her eyes at the clownish Michele but soon discovered that our staff jacket wasn't entirely waterproof. During a downpour, Nina taped four black garbage bags together to construct an intricate parka with a hole for her head, making her look like a decrepit bag lady rather than a stylish young Italian woman. On top of it she wrote in masking tape and black marker, "*Non sono un sacco nero. No buttarmi via!*" (I'm not a black trash bag. Don't throw me away!). She told me that she brought her worst clothes to camp. "At the end of the summer, I just throw them all in the garbage or burn them!"

One day I wore a shirt with an actual collar—an old dress shirt that was nearly worn out.

"Wow, Dario!" Martina says. "What's the occasion? Why are you all dressed up?"

The one Italian staff member who never dressed down and was ready for anything was Sergio. Besides his pocket-filled vest, he wore a wide utility belt with loops, snaps, and pockets to carry all his gadgets in case he was left to fend for himself against the wolves and bears. The campers nicknamed it the "*cintura di avventura,*" or adventure belt, but he sensed their envy and knew they'd be coming to him in their most desperate hour when the cougars came in for the kill.

During an outing at the headwaters at the Mississippi River, I assured the staff that wild animals were the least of their problems in the forests of Minnesota. I warned them that the biggest dangers are the ticks, mosquitoes, and poison ivy. Letizia searched the Italian-English dictionary for a translation of the three-leafed poisonous herb. None of the Italians had ever heard of it.

Sergio assumed we were playing a prank when I showed him this seemingly innocuous little vine. "What? You expect me to believe that if I took this plant and rubbed it all over my body that I could end up in the hospital?"

To show he was not afraid, he reached down to pick the stem so he could rub the leaves all over his face. I grabbed him by the waist and pulled him back, trying to save him from himself. Still, he struggled to grab the poison ivy so he could prove me wrong. He finally backed off. After this incident I was convinced that these Italians didn't stand a chance in the north woods.

Sergio showed me that he had lotion on his adventure belt that would cure any of these ailments. For a mountain man, he was surprisingly coy about roughing it. The American staff took off their shoes to run through the ankle-deep water at the headwaters of the Mississippi. Sergio reluctantly followed suit, but as we strolled downstream, he complained repeatedly about the round pebbles of the riverbed irritating his toes. Finally, Elisabetta from Nebraska yelled, "If you will please just stop your whining, I'll go get your shoes." She walked the quarter mile back to fetch his boots as he sat back, content that she was doing this all for him. I mistakenly thought this outing would build staff unity, but divisions were forming.

We roasted hotdogs over a campfire. Most of the Italians were adapting to getting their clothes dirty in the woods and eating casually rather than enjoying a typical three-course Italian dinner. Sergio, however, preferred not to sit down on a log, where he might get his clothes dirty. When a drop of ketchup fell from the bun onto his utility vest, he jumped and issued an impressive stream of Italian swearwords.

"Oh please . . ." Elisabetta responded annoyed.

Sergio was ready for anything, including soiled clothes. He deftly wiped away the excess ketchup with a handkerchief, whipped out a Spray 'n Wash laundry stick from one of his pockets, and dabbed the soap onto the stain.

He looked up at the rest of us staring at him and advised, "Always be prepared."

During orientation, Linda, the jolly health care authority for all the language camps, told me that we were having trouble finding enough nurses for all the camps. I asked her, "Do we really need a nurse on-site all the time?"

"You better believe it, Dario!" she responded enthusiastically. "We need to keep those whippersnickers safe!" The health and safety orientation that Linda gave for the new staff terrified many of the first-year counselors, who thought they had signed up just to have fun with the kids. Our American staff had to translate for the Italians, who up until that time thought they knew English well. But Linda had her own slang.

The native Italians were already wary of guns and violence in America, then they got advice about what to do if an "active shooter" was at camp. Then they were terrified. It didn't help that BSU rented one of its empty dormitories to the local SWAT team for drills. The shell-shocked Italians stepped out of these sessions only to find policemen in full military armor with facemasks and submachine guns running into another building. Letizia assured them that this was just a drill and we were supposed to just ignore them. Sergio wasn't scared in the least and started clicking photos to show friends back home. One of the masked policeman pulled him aside and made him delete all the images, but not before Sergio could admire the weapons up close.

I had to talk down many of these nervous newbies, who thought that we'd be hauling kids out on stretchers and scraping dead ones off the floor. "If we're careful, everything should be fine," I assured them.

Then I watched as our five junior counselors fell apart during orientation before the campers had even arrived. Liliana got rock slivers lodged in her sole, and Gaia showed up with a broken leg, determined to make it through more than a month of camp on crutches. The second evening of orientation, Matteo, dressed as an attractive Cleopatra for a skit, rushed Jessica to the nurse after she fell hard on her arm. I drove her to the emergency room and spent the night with her as she recovered from having her dislocated elbow put back in its socket.

The day before the kids arrived, Tiziana had a terrifying allergic reaction to a bee sting. As her throat was closing up, I jabbed her leg with a needle of epinephrine, loaded her into my little Honda, and sped her to the clinic. I had another EpiPen ready to jam into her thigh if she fell asleep and stopped breathing. On the hour drive, she kept dozing off, so I blasted the sound track from *South Park*, and the expletives of the cartoon characters kept her awake. I then understood the logic of having a nurse always available. However, it's just as important to have an extra staff member, usually Zeta, ready to drive the wounded to the clinic.

To be accredited for safety standards, the camp had to pass the American Camp Association guidelines. We were forced to take down the swings because we didn't have a thick, contained layer of wood chips or ground-up tires to soften the fall of those campers spilling off the swings. In other words, if there's any chance that someone could get hurt, shut it down.

When the camp started in the 1920s, a high dive was built far out in the lake so kids could practice their backflips from thirty feet in the air. This had been disassembled because of insurance worries. And we had a lifeguard watching over kids even in just a foot of water. Scott, the camp's caretaker, laughed when he saw our lifeguard at the Mississippi headwaters in six inches of water with his whistle and tube ready to rescue our teenaged campers. He said, "There were toddlers running through the creek, and there was Luigi the lifeguard with his rescue tube. I don't think that tube would even float in that much water and would probably just get in the way of trying to haul someone out." Still, rules are rules.

Before the kids arrived, we performed a "missing camper drill," although it was highly unlikely that any camper would venture away from the group since they were terrified of being gobbled up by hungry bears. One year, Tiziana volunteered to be the guinea pig "missing camper" for our drill and viewed this as a great chance to tan in the sun in her American flag bikini and read her book. I told her not to hide too well, since this was just practice for the real thing.

She walked out the long road down the isthmus with a lake on either side toward the entrance to the camp property. Rather than just stay on the road, she ventured a bit into the woods, but the mosquitoes ate at her bare flesh. She stepped into the water to splash away the bugs, but her flip-flops got stuck in the mud. When she reached down to free her sandals, she noticed a decomposing fish. Disgusted, she crawled out of the water up into a tree, wondering when someone would save her. Her stomach gurgled from the stench, and she realized she shouldn't have eaten an entire plate of bacon for breakfast followed by a lunch of another plate of bacon. Still in the tree, she lost both meals all over the ground below her but somehow didn't fall out of the tree. When no one found her, she returned to camp, warning others not to go out there. Perhaps that was the best result of the drill.

GOOD IMPRESSIONS ON OPENING DAY

"Never let two buses meet. You have to have someone at the gate warning the first bus to wait until the other one leaves," the caretaker of our site, Scott, warned me about the single-lane, dirt road into our Italian immersion camp. Scott's family had run the site for generations and had worked hard to keep it pristine. "A couple of years ago, two trucks met and took an hour and a half to back up, while all the other cars waited. It was not pretty." I surveyed the branches of cedar trees reaching out to touch each other across the narrow isthmus between two lakes. If a bus swerved even slightly, it would drop down into the water.

As the dean of the camp, I took note of this along with dozens of details about how to run a smooth opening day: the moment when the buses and cars arrive with all the campers. We were scrambling to finish setting up before the arrival of the campers later that day.

We wanted to make a good impression on the parents as they rolled into camp to leave their kids for a couple of weeks. The camp was in a classic setting on a peninsula with two lakes visible from most anywhere and cabins perched on stilts on hills above the shore. While I thought this was a bit of paradise, I knew the kids could be terror stricken as they were often facing their first overnight experience without their parents. "Remember that parents will often come early, so we should be ready," Lucrezia reminded the staff, who were in high spirits and excited to meet these kids.

Two buses full of kids and minivans with parents were due in two hours, so I hoisted the Italian flag up the pole to embolden us as we transformed our site into a Little Italy where we would speak only Italian. The first half of the summer, a French camp had occupied the site, so they had just cleaned the camp and lowered the French flag.

The French had made friends with the animals at this rustic site and had been perhaps a bit too friendly. Besides the mice scurrying around in search of any morsel (they are not as cute as in *Ratatouille*), we discovered a far-too-friendly chipmunk who lived in the staff house whom the French had named "George" or "*petit Suisse*," little Swiss, because his stripes looked like the Swiss guards' at the Vatican. He had stolen four pounds of peanut butter M&Ms in one day from the French staff, and now he ran right up to our feet in search of more.

The Italian staff were not pleased. Sergio started setting traps, which were soon snapping away and catching hungry mice. A contest ensued as to who could catch the most mice (I caught fifteen in my cabin but lost to the nurse, who caught one every day for a month). Still, these traps were too small for the chubby chipmunk in the staff house and his fat friend who snuck into the dining hall.

"Dario, I need you to go into town to get cash for the villagers when they arrive," Lucrezia told me. All the kids exchange their dollars for Euros, as a tourist in Italy would, so we needed to make proper change for the parents. I protested that we still weren't ready for the kids to arrive, but Lucrezia didn't have a driver's license, and I was the only other person whose name was on the bank account. "We'll be fine," she assured me, and I raced into town, not to return for almost an hour.

My cell phone jingled in my pocket as I walked into the bank. It was Luca, the head cook. "There's a guy here to inspect us," he said almost happily. "Here, I'll put him on."

"Hi there!" a jolly man yelled. I held the phone away from my ear and still heard him say, "I'm from the Minnesota Department of Health, and it's that time of year for a surprise inspection."

I paused for a moment wondering if this was a summer camp prank. How should I play it? Could this be Salvatore the baker, a notorious joker who "accidentally" ran off with the van keys the day before, leaving us hours behind in setup. "Oh really?" I replied. "And you want to inspect us?"

"Yup. I stop by every year. I was up in Brainerd, so I thought I'd poke around to see what I can find. Your cook here can show me around until you get back. See ya!"

He had to be legit. But why now? Could he close down our camp before we even got started?

I zoomed back to camp with just an hour to spare before we officially opened the gates to parents. I stopped in the kitchen to find the inspector and Luca chatting away merrily. That had to be a good sign. Luca wore a leather tricorn hat and usually sported a skull-and-crossbones T-shirt. Today, though, he had on his green Oscar the Grouch shirt, which wasn't fitting, because he was in an exceptionally jolly mood, which was perfect for keeping the inspector distracted.

"The only problem here is you have to keep that chipmunk out of the dining hall," the inspector warned Luca gently. *Good, he probably won't shut our doors,* I thought. The inspector and I set out to inspect the rest of the camp.

Strange . . . the business office was empty, and no one was setting anything up for opening day. This was not good.

The inspector and I walked by the beach, where Lucrezia and a few others were putting on their clothes over their wet underwear as some fisherman trolled by in their Lund boats, very interested in the unfolding scene. What on earth was going on?

"We're all pissed," one of the counselors told me in Italian so the inspector couldn't understand. "The lifeguards decided to do another missing villager drill while you were in town, so we all had to stop everything and search." The spotters had to take off their clothes immediately to comb the bottom of the lake for the fake camper. The reasoning was that if a villager were truly missing, they wouldn't have time to go back to their cabins to put on their swimsuits. They'd have to strip on the spot.

"What a beautiful site you have here," the inspector told me, oblivious to the seminude staffers and the drooling fishermen.

The rest of the disgruntled counselors spread out across the campsite and reported back through the crackle of their walkietalkies. Sergio then shouted into the radio in Italian, "My god, there's blood everywhere! What a mess!" He had taken advantage of the relative calm during the search to corner the fat chipmunk in the staff house and bludgeon it with a log. "How do you clean up all this blood? Does anyone have any bleach?"

Fortunately, the inspector didn't understand Italian, so I carefully steered him away from the staff house. I was both repulsed and pleased to be rid of the chipmunk, but why hadn't Sergio used a live trap and why right now? This northern Italian was very pleased with his handiwork. I told him over the walkie-talkie that once he'd cleaned up the gore and washed the blood from his hands, perhaps that was a good time to go to the gate to greet guests.

He walked out of the staff house with a big grin (and no visible blood). He cheerily greeted the inspector, who told us as he left that the only issue at camp was the chipmunk in the dining hall. "No problem," Sergio told us, "I can take care of it for you."

"No, really," I responded. "Thanks, but we'll just plug the holes where he gets inside."

"I just want to be helpful," Sergio responded and went to the gate with his walkie-talkie to direct the cars so they wouldn't meet on the one-lane road.

Too late. A couple of cars with campers were already parking almost an hour ahead of schedule and probably witnessed the beach blanket bingo. I greeted the parents, who apologized for their early arrival. I assured them we'd be ready for them at two o'clock and in the meantime they were welcome to wander around the site—fortunately, the staff house had a large *Vietato l'ingresso* (do not enter) sign, and the spotters at the beach were mostly clothed.

Just then, a gleaming white Toyota Celica, the "action package" model, zoomed into camp, and Zeta, the assistant dean, stepped out. From Martina's, Lucrezia's, and Letizia's descriptions, I was expecting Zeta to be flashy, brash, and controlling. Instead she was small, blonde, and polite. She greeted everyone shyly and instantly fit right in. Somehow all the other counselors trusted her and confided their secrets to her. Now we were ready for the campers to arrive.

The missing villager drill was over, and the staff rallied to get everything in place to check in the new campers and prepare for the two buses full of nervous *bambini*. From the parking lot, a Neapolitan named Fabio spoke on the staticky walkie-talkie to Sergio, who hailed from the far north, at the gate to prevent cars from meeting on the single-lane road. In true southern-Italian fashion Fabio constantly teased the far-too-serious northerner, who accidentally let both buses pass. A fatal mistake.

Scott stumbled back in panic when I told him the news of the problem, caused by this north-south rift. The Neapolitan was unfazed and comforted him, "No problem. I've seen far worse in

Napoli. Sometimes buses even get wedged between buildings back home. Here, there is much space." He expertly guided one of the buses backwards as the other enormous coach slid by with inches to spare. The bus drivers thanked the Neapolitan traffic expert as kids flooded off the bus to cheers of "*Ben arrivati!*" from the staff. Even the anxious caretaker was impressed.

I sat down and said, "All of this, and the campers have only just arrived..."

Fabio promised, "Don't worry, we can handle anything."

MOTHER DUCK

KIDS ENTERING THE ITALIAN IMMERSION CAMP GO THROUGH our passport control, change their dollars for Euros, and open their bags for customs, all in Italian. They choose an Italian-sounding name to help them become a new person at camp. Most important, though, they say good-bye to Mom. The first day or two, the culture shock is so intense that they generally don't have a big emotional reaction. Then the nostalgia di casa, or "nostalgia for home," kicks in. Homesickness can be an intense "illness," or as little Chiara pointed out, "I hope I'm not as homesick this year. Last year, I cried half the time, but I only cry every once in a while now."

At breakfast one morning while we were eating our granola and bran flakes, little Edoardo went pale. He'd been quiet since he arrived, but now he seemed different. He set down his spoon into his empty bowl, and the cereal from inside his stomach came right back up. Marina dutifully sprinkled the "Wheaties" packet of sawdust over the mess on the floor as the others decided they'd had enough cereal for today.

Suddenly, everything from home was better, especially the food. The homesickness spread. Giuseppina, who was ten, told us, "If you ever go to D.C., there's a really great cupcake place you should go to. Except my mom's cupcakes are better." Tears welled up in her eyes as she explained, "Not just because I like her, but because they are better."

Katy, my wife, and our three-year-old daughter, Stellina, were with me at camp, and I worried about managing the camp with a toddler constantly wanting my attention. But Stellina waddled up to little homesick girls, beaming with happiness. After seeing Stellina, Giuseppina took a deep sigh and said, "I'm OK now. If she can do it, so can I."

Stellina's charm didn't work on all the kids, though. Elisabettina, who was twelve and "a terror," according to Tiziana, acted tough and unmoved when her cabinmates missed home. To frighten them into submission, she declared, "When my parents ask me what I want for breakfast, I say, 'your soul.'" (After a few days, her parents picked her up. She was scaring the other kids by speaking in tongues and rarely displaying emotion, but she was also terribly homesick.)

On the third day, which we call *il giorno della nostalgia,* or "homesickness day," many kids hit rock bottom. Little Sandrino asked us to mail a letter home that read: "Dear Mom, I would like it if you called in and asked to pick me up early. I don't like [the] food, bugs. I don't like any one."

Letizia had an action plan: "Dario, you have to dress up as Cleopatra to make it all better!" That evening we reenacted the murder of Julius Caesar by the Roman senators, and I put on an itchy black wig and ridiculous sequined dress to perform as a hideous Cleopatra with a baritone voice. Caesar was played by Cesare, a Harvard-educated genius who had never been to Italy but spoke such grammatically perfect Italian that the native speakers listened in awe. As a macho Cleopatra, I bullied the henpecked, skinny Caesar. Seeing the dean of the camp in drag made even the most homesick kid snicker and forget mamma's cupcakes for a while. I stood over the body of Caesar—bloodied with the best Heinz ketchup—and wept in mock outrage. The kids whipped out their digital cameras, and their flashes lit up the evening. *Great*, I thought, *now they'll go home and tell their parents, "This is our dean!"*

The dean of the Swedish camp had told me that she had banned all cross-dressing because it's essentially misogynist. I countered, saying that it makes fun of our stereotypical idea of overly effeminate women, and noted that sometimes women dress up as men and make fun of the supermacho guy who only grunts. Isn't this all just making fun of gender roles? What about Shakespeare's all-male casts?

Soon crazy costumes and cross-dressing became part of most skits since everyone assumed a new identity. Cesare added a glitzy feather boa to his toga outfit and proclaimed, "I suddenly feel so liberated! I think I'll wear this all the time."

The cathartic bloodletting from killing Caesar relieved kids' homesickness for the moment, but they still wrote emotion-filled letters to their parents demanding to be rescued immediately. We encouraged them to make their moms a great piece of art to express their feelings. To demonstrate their undying love for Mom, they worked feverishly on arts-and-crafts projects imitating great Renaissance masterpieces, constructing with yarn, paper plates, lanyards, and lots of glue. By the time the parents received the letters or came to pick up their kids, the homesickness had long since passed. The youngsters unceremoniously passed on the *Last Supper* in Popsicle sticks to their parents, not wanting to make a scene in front of their peers. Often, the priceless artwork had taken a beating from being stuffed into a suitcase—along with clothes splotched with acrylic paint and Elmer's glue.

If melancholy strikes again, some of the kids make themselves physically ill with homesickness and demand to call their moms. Speaking to their parents upsets them more, so they are allowed to talk to their parents only if it's an emergency. They sometimes check themselves into the infirmary, where the nurse speaks English, and she checks in with the parents. This break from the chaos of camp often puts the kids at ease, and their disease is miraculously "cured"—at least until the next visit to the nurse.

One of the campers, Annina, managed to trick two different nurses into letting her call home. When the nurse stepped out of the clinic for five minutes to put out hand-washing buckets for lunch, Annina again pounced on the phone and called her mom to tell her about a simulation about immigration we were doing. The panicked mother called every one of my bosses, demanding that we "stop segregating some of the kids just to yell at them."

She finally got me on the phone and told me, "I've seen the studies of these simulations, and they are psychologically damaging. Her therapist does not think this is a good idea, and I demand it stop immediately!" I assured her that no such emotional abuse was taking place, but she continued to believe her daughter was trapped in a dangerous situation and wanted to pull her out early.

I returned to the group, shaken by the confrontation, and saw Annina playing happily with her friends. During the debriefing, she offered interesting perspectives on what she learned during the simulation and was oblivious to the trouble her phone call had caused.

During our staff meeting the next day, I pointed out that we needed to spare the nurse visits from the kids who mostly wanted to speak English, by repeating ourselves very slowly in simple Italian and using lots of gestures to make sure they understood. I said that we wanted to avoid the power imbalance between those who understood everything and those who were beginners. Or as little Umberto said, "I feel like I'm playing charades and losing!"

To help the kids comprehend, we often repeated everything three to thirty times and used emphatic gestures and sounds. Michele took this to heart and had taken to just making noises with his cabin of seven- to nine-year-old boys. He told them to roar like Chewbacca from *Star Wars* or screech like pterodactyls.

"You have no idea how annoying that is," said Nina to the cabin of shrieking dinosaurs as everyone covered their ears. Still, his campers adored him and followed him like little ducklings. They didn't need their parents—they'd found their mother duck.

NINJAS VERSUS PIRATES

I'D HEARD FROM THE STAFF THAT THE PREVIOUS ITALIAN DEAN ran the camp with an iron fist, which they despised but somehow respected. I realized I did enjoy running the camp and tried to make it a fun camp for the staff and kids where everyone had input. Martina took a different view, "You know, Dario, you have to yell at the staff sometimes to let them know who's in charge."

I was confused. Essentially Martina was asking me to yell at her. I responded, "If I have to scream at you and the rest of the counselors to make you respect me, I really don't want to do this job." She shook her head, not convinced I'd succeed.

I explained that especially with the campers we should avoid raising our voices because it just increased the volume level and then no one was happy. I told the staff that the best way to get the kids' attention was to speak quietly or use little games like rhythmic clapping for them to repeat. The returning staff seemed to think I had a lot to learn, and besides, my plan wasn't "very Italian."

I laid out my vision for a more democratic camp. "I know you're not paid much for this twenty-four-hour-a-day job, so I at least want you to own your activities."

Luisa, who was half-Swiss and half-American, wasn't so sure.

She was tired of guessing what I wanted. "Can't you just tell us what to do?"

I explained that I could give her guidance, but I wanted to set a framework and then have the counselors use their imaginations. She was still not satisfied.

"OK," I replied, exasperated. "Go get me some coffee."

"Right away!" she hopped to her feet and made me a delicious cappuccino. Perhaps fascism is underrated.

Lucrezia explained, "All we want are specific rules that we can follow." I countered that life isn't that way, and she was definitely not satisfied with that response because she thought I was just trying to get out of making decisions. I explained that we had definite rules on safety, but many others were guidelines about which we as a group had to come to a consensus.

I knew that the counselors, some who were just a couple of years older than the kids, wanted absolute authority so they could maintain control. At the same time, each one wanted to be the most fun and loved counselor of all. This was where my job seemed to be to relax their strict rules so as to not turn camp into a police state. I didn't want to relive the Stanford prison experiment in the north woods. The counselors needed to convince the kids rather than just demand they follow them.

The native Italians appreciated the more laid-back style. I hoped it would encourage creativity. Carlotta from Sicily wanted to take it a step further. She pointed to our daily schedule pasted on the back of the kids' name tags. "This would never happen in Italy. Never." She didn't like the hectic agenda ruled by the clock, "Everything should be more *easy* and *relax*." I got the idea that any schedule was too confining to her.

To encourage cooperation, I asked the staff to be patient with each other, especially if someone was running late, because who knows what issues they had with the kids? Slowly we lessened and lengthened the number of activities. The rhythm was more "easy" and less frantic. "You should never let your schedule rule you," Carlotta advised.

I thought Sergio believed I was giving too much power to the counselors, so he wanted to make sure that everyone stayed on task. He handed out walkie-talkies to the staff so they could instantly communicate and properly manage any situation. Cell phone reception was spotty in the north woods, so these two-way radios would keep him in constant contact with everyone. He imparted his knowledge of proper transmission protocol to the staff, who had stopped listening to him long ago. "You must always keep it on," he advised. "You must begin saying who you are and whom you are calling. You must . . . You must . . ." The restless staff listened politely, but when he left, they promptly turned off their walkie-talkies.

I carried my walkie-talkie with me around camp and mostly heard Sergio asking if anyone was listening to him. In general the staff didn't use their walkie-talkies, but I realized that most of them did in fact have them on when a report came in from the soccer field that two penalty kicks that shouldn't have been called were against the Italians so we lost the game to the Germans. Fortunately the kids were calm, but the staff were steaming.

We invited the Germans and the French to our camp for a Swiss Day celebration, and I knew that I had to be exceptionally organized for these groups because they were used to far more structure. I planned a giant four-way capture-the-flag match that represented the four languages of Switzerland: German, French, Italian, and Romansh. I divided the camp with caution cones and presented each team with a map delineating the borders. I explained the detailed rules (which were translated into French and German): If a team captured another's flag, that territory would be annexed. Then those two teams were united to go after the other two teams' flags.

I figured that the Italian staff would be pleased by all these exhaustive rules. During the game, the German team soon captured both the French and Italian flags, which made these three groups into one team against the small Romansh area. The Italians, however, viewed the Germans taking their flag as an occupation, not a unification, despite the rules. The counselors Cesare and Paolo turned partisan and worked for the Romansh rather than the Germans. They proudly sang the partisan anthem "Bella Ciao!" but another Italian counselor, Michele, protested that we should never brainwash the kids with this Communist propaganda.

Cesare and Paolo tried to convince some of the French to join them, as if the traitorous Vichy government was in power. They liberated Romansh prisoners and tried to help them find the German flag. Even so, the overwhelming numbers of the three teams led the Germans to an easy victory over the poor Romansh.

I laughed when I heard about the plot to overthrow the "occupying government," but some of the counselors accused them of not following the rules. "Where would we be if the partisans 'followed the rules' in World War II?" they countered. Fortunately, it was time for our Swiss dinner of spaetzle and heavy, creamed pork.

During the first week of camp, I watched the staff give all their energy despite not understanding how everything was supposed to work. The smooth second week flew by, but by the time the third week hit, all the counselors were either sick or angry. Little feuds erupted over such minor annoyances as the off-key singing of a reworked Mexican melody about bussing dishes. I advised the staff to take a deep breath and move on.

As the staff became harder to manage, the campers presented an even bigger challenge. Sweet eight-year-old Angioletta—whose name does in fact mean "little angel"—showed Letizia a photo of her "enemy."

"*You* have an enemy? I thought you liked everyone." Letizia asked.

"Oh no! I have many of them . . . she's the fourth."

We never understood how Angioletta got a photo of her enemy but soon learned not to cross her.

Fifteen-year-old Mario was the camp clown and would do anything to make a joke. After days of his frenetic hijinks and constant banter, the Argentine counselor, Vale, couldn't stand it anymore. She told Mario that if he couldn't keep with the program, she'd tie him to the cross in the chapel to keep him from moving.

I told Vale, "I think some of the Christians would be kind of upset."

"Oh, I never even thought of that!" Vale responded. In retaliation, Mario pretended to be the crucified Spartacus, the slave leader who rebelled against the Roman oppression. Vale was not amused.

The little girls from another cabin were especially rambunctious, and little Assunta yelled at her counselor, Gabriella, "You can't tell me what to do; you're not my mom!" Gabriella, who Matteo dubbed the camp's Julia Roberts, sighed because she always ended up with little girls that either cried from homesickness or refused to cooperate. She explained that all of them just needed to clean the cabin, but Isabella backed up her friend Assunta, "Yeah, I have human rights!" But Gabriella started cleaning, and eventually they all joined in.

These little girls all wanted to go to the restroom at the same time, especially during dinner. Since we couldn't deny them bathrooms, the staff strategized and sent them with another person at the table who wasn't their best friend. Incredibly, they were back in the dining hall within minutes.

Matteo from Rome wanted, like all the others, to be the favorite counselor at camp and figured out how to convince the kids to follow: he did away with passive activities such as braiding bracelets and painting rocks. No one signed up for my activity of "Documents with Dario" to learn how to navigate Italian bureaucracy ("The Romans invented it; the Italians perfected it!"). Matteo went along with Tiziana's plan to prepare a battle between ninjas and pirates—with the two of them as the leaders. Letizia warned them about "regressive pull": when counselors get roped into acting like preteens to impress the campers through unwise activities such as milk-drinking contests. Matteo seemed sure this wouldn't happen to him. Besides, the head cook, Luca, had already hoisted a Jolly Roger flag in the kitchen and wore a tricorn pirate's hat while he cooked. He would gladly play along with the game.

Matteo and Tiziana dressed up their kids with black headbands, and they sneaked around the camp stealthily. They hung up dozens of ninja posters proclaiming "NINJA!!!" deep in the pirate territory of the dining hall. Other counselors complained to me that this was too intrusive when they were eating and that the activity excluded those not in the ninja group. When I failed to see how this was hurting anyone, the disgruntled counselors once again thought I was far too permissive.

Meanwhile during the activity period, the ninjas slinked around camp "spying" on other groups playing volleyball or painting in the arts-and-crafts house. The little secret agents giggled with delight about how sneaky they were, while the counselors leading the other activities became annoyed. Tiziana and Matteo's ninjas crept up to the little kitchen where Gabriella was leading the activity of making fresh pasta. The kids hid in the bushes and peered through the windows at the other campers calmly cooking *tagliatelle*. Then, Tiziana grabbed a utensil and ran off with the group of little bandits.

I was in the business office overlooking this scene and suddenly the walkie-talkies, which no one had agreed to use, blazed to life. "A villager has stolen a knife and is now running away," Gabriella reported from the kitchen. Immediately, the other staff assumed the worst: a villager with a giant cleaver was on a murderous rampage. I didn't know exactly what had happened, but we caught the rebel ninjas. The other counselors shouted that the leaders, Tiziana and Matteo, were endangering everyone by encouraging stealing and giving weapons to the kids. Tiziana and Matteo didn't understand what the fuss was about.

During our staff meeting, I let both sides shout as they loudly complained about each other. I told them if the campers saw that the staff was divided, we were finished. Then I quietly said that we should give the ninjas a rest and perhaps offer a different activity now. The pirates were pacified, thanks to Letizia, who formed an activity group with them. Livia, who had also been a counselor at the Japanese camp, sent the spirit of the ninjas back to Japan. Neither side was completely content, as they wanted punishments doled out. But mostly the staff forgot about the controversy, and some were soon talking about the imminent zombie apocalypse.

NOT SO POLITICALLY CORRECT

MARCO POLO ARRIVED AT THE BEACH THE FIRST EVENING, HAVing lost his way to Cathay. Dressed as the Venetian explorer, Nico, a witty, blond counselor from near the Swiss border, docked his canoe and took off his life jacket (safety first). The campers gathered at the waterfront informed him that he had landed at an Italian summer camp, not in China. This is how we opened camp the first evening, giving Polo a tour of the site as a way to explain how everything worked. Nico insisted that he'd arrived in China, and he pulled back his eyes to look more Asian. Letizia and I looked at each other and cringed at his gesture; fortunately it caused no conflict.

Nico had no idea that this could be construed as offensive when Letizia mentioned it. Thinking Americans were overly sensitive, Nina from Torino said that Italy has a long tradition of funny put-downs. She gave us an example: "He's got such a big nose that when he nods, he slices bread, and when he shakes his head, he clears the table." Or if someone is overweight, they say, "He's so short and fat that it's easier to jump on his head than run around him."

"You Americans need to lighten up," said Carlo, a quick-witted retired computer executive from Taranto, who had volunteered with his wife to build a pizza oven. He could barely fit inside the nearly completed oven to finish the grout, and he criticized Americans kids for eating like savages. "They hold their knives and forks with their fists like they're going to kill someone!"

The Italian staff tried to be careful since they understood how sensitive Americans can be, but then the counselors Luigi and Simone had it come back against them. They were washing their clothes at the Laundromat in town when they heard a mother arguing with and swearing at her son. To avoid an embarrassing situation, Simone spoke in Italian to Luigi. The son heard this mysterious language and said to his mom, "I don't understand what they're saying. Are they terrorists?" She replied that she didn't know whether they were Al-Qaeda or not, and she kept her son away from the suspicious foreigners.

Simone was disgusted, but the ever-patient Luigi addressed them, "We're speaking Italian. Do you know where Italy is? It's in Europe. Do you think you could find it on a map?" They just stared at him, perhaps a bit embarrassed that he understood everything they had said.

Despite these attempts to break down barriers, the one blinding prejudice many of the Italians couldn't seem to get over was their opinions of the Germans. In spite of our annual Swiss Day celebrations with the French at the German camp, our native Italian staff didn't feel any connection to their neighbors to the north. "Dario," Nina told me, "you must understand that we are completely different. There is no connection here at all." I reminded her that in southern Switzerland—Lugano, Bellinzona—they speak Italian. "That means nothing," Nina said dismissively. Sergio clarified that the Spanish, Portuguese, and Greeks are "cousins," but the Germans and Swiss are a "different species. Really!"

I'd already had some experience at the site of the relatively posh German camp when I had pulled together an Italian weekend for adults in the off-season. I knew that adults claim they want "full immersion," just like our regular summer camp, but they really don't. They are used to understanding everything and can't stand it when unintelligible prattle flits by them.

Most of the usual counselors were back at college, so my friend Mike recommended Daniella, who taught cooking and Italian classes to adults in Minneapolis. After I hired her, another Italian in Minneapolis commented, "I hope you know what you're in for. She's from Napoli, you know." I'd forgotten that many Italians not only have strong biases against northern Europeans but also have prejudices against other Italians.

Soon, though, I realized what was meant. Daniella refused to drive in Minnesota because we're "lazy drivers" compared to her fellow Neapolitans back home. "They may be crazy drivers in Napoli, but at least they're awake!" Her thick accent and criticism of all things American made me think she'd just gotten off the boat, but during our trip north I found out that she had been here for twelve years. She'd just chosen not to conform to our silly ways, which worried me. After listening to her rant against Americans, I hoped that she'd sleep or at least be quiet for a bit on the long ride. Instead, she deemed it her duty to talk nonstop for the five-hour drive.

In spite of my worries, she was fantastic with the adults. The other counselors had a difficult transition from rounding up kids and making sure no one was missing to offering learning opportunities to adults. Daniella understood that most adults want to skip the song and dance routines and are happy just conjugating verbs all day.

Along with the adults, she didn't want a strict schedule, wanting it to be more "Italian." In fact, she refused to even look at the agenda I'd arranged for the weekend. I handed her the printed program, but she turned her head and wouldn't look at it. "Why are you doing this?" I insisted.

"Look, Dario, it is hard enough for me to be at a German camp." She then sat down as though she was suffering from trauma. "Now if I have to look at your schedule—if I even have to look at a watch while I'm here, I'll feel like I'm in a *lager*."

I was speechless that she felt like this was a prison.

Regardless of her extreme views, the adult campers adored her quirkiness and candor, but each time we had a new activity, I had to find her since she refused to look at a clock.

For our grand banquet on the last evening, Daniella taught everyone how to roll out homemade pasta. The cook, who wisely didn't inform her that he usually cooks German food, had already realized that Daniella would control the menu completely.

"Dario, we need *vino* for the meal tonight," she commanded me. "Can you get some red, white, and then *spumante* or *moscato* for afterwards?"

I told her that alcohol wasn't allowed at camp, but she just laughed. "You have an *Italian* weekend without wine? Good one!"

I insisted that I would lose my job if I brought in bottles of wine.

"You aren't very Italian, Dario," she scolded.

Just then, my boss, Denise, entered the dining hall to see how the weekend was going. Daniella confronted her, saying that these people had paid for an Italian experience and we must be allowed some wine or at least some *prosecco* before dinner. Denise calmly explained that this was against policy.

I watch as Daniella demanded wine, and Denise just as firmly, but politely, clarified the rules.

Realizing she was getting nowhere, Daniella turned to me and said in Italian, "She's another one of those Germans, no?"

Denise likely understood but maintained her composure. I told Daniella that Denise actually had a French background, and Daniella viewed it a travesty that someone who was French couldn't bend the rules for some wine. The adult campers had caught on to the conversation and obviously wanted Daniella to win the argument. We started eating as the futile discussion continued. Denise finally broke free of the stalemate and wished us "*bon appetit!*" Daniella went into the kitchen to check on the main course.

She discovered that the cook used wine for cooking, so she examined the bottle. "Ugh, I wouldn't even use this in sauce!" She then noticed that the cook was allowed to add some liquor to desserts such as *tiramisù*.

I had stepped outside for a minute to talk with Denise, and by the time I returned, Daniela had commandeered a bottle of Kahlúa and had given each happy adult a healthy dose poured over a dollop of vanilla *gelato*.

The cook watched the scene, and I caught his eye in search of an explanation. "Well, this is technically OK according to the camp rules," he shrugged.

The adult campers were thrilled. Daniella was a hero! She looked at me proudly, "We'll teach these Germans how to have fun yet!"

"FRIENDSHIP" TOURNAMENT

Even though I'm not Italian, I've learned to accept Italian pride. The Italian staff at the language camp would have probably agreed that vanity is one of the seven deadly sins, but it wasn't easy for these passionate Mediterraneans to suppress their emotions when they were surrounded by stoic Norwegian Americans like myself.

Sergio couldn't resist shouting at the staff of the French language camp, "Thieves! Give us back the *Mona Lisa!*" I attempted to calm him by explaining that the Italians stole the Val d'Aosta region from France, and many people there still speak French. "Yes," he replied, "but they are much happier now that they are part of Italy."

Many of the native Italian staff were quick to complain about their government, its bureaucracy, and the resulting corruption but never questioned the country's dominance in art, food, or soccer. Roberto informed me, "Did you know that Italy has the most masterpieces of any country? Far more than France." I knew better than to suggest that *masterpiece* is a subjective term.

During our week of orientation, we typically take a field trip to the site where we will set up our Italian camp. The French camp is on the site at the beginning of the summer, and the French counselors graciously host us for the day before we move in to their site over the weekend. Still, I was nervous of an impending Franco-Italo war of words.

I was aware before this visit of important soccer history. Italy had won the World Cup several years before (we don't talk about the losing years), and Italian friends took this as a personal victory. I suggested that "the Italian national team won," but they corrected me: "*We* won the World Cup." They could easily ignore that the brilliantly talented but hot-headed Marco Materazzi insulted the sister of French player Zinedine Zidane, who famously head-butted him and was expelled, causing France to lose. "If the referee hadn't handed him a red card, we would have attacked France," an Italian friend told me seriously.

Not wanting the seemingly irrelevant World Cup to boil over into summer language camp, I advised my staff to be on their best behavior during our visit with the French staff. I asked them to please leave the World Cup behind and not bring that hostility to the French camp. One of the staff rebutted, "You want us to ignore soccer? How do you think we can do that?"

Fortunately, the French staff didn't broach the prickly soccer issue and treated us to a tasty lunch of *salade niçoise*. Art thievery stayed out of the discussions, as did historical land grabs, and I was pleased to see the French and Italian staff quickly becoming friends.

Perhaps trying to divert any animosity, a French counselor asked if the Italian camp was going to build a wood-fire pizza oven like the German camp's.

"What?" demanded Matteo from Rome. "Why do they have a pizza oven? Pizza isn't German."

To further fuel the outrage (and perhaps dodge a bullet), the French staff pointed out that the German village also had Nutella every morning and many of them claimed that this chocolate-hazelnut spread was invented by wise chocolatiers in the land of chocolate: Germany.

"Ignorance!" Sergio exclaimed. "Of course we Italians are happy to share our food with the world, but we all know that Nutella, a very *Italian* name, was dreamed up by a genius from my region: Piemonte!"

Perhaps egging on the irritated Italians, one of the French cooks mentioned that the Spanish camp has a welcoming dinner of *spaghetti bolognese* and the Swedish camp has special pizza delivery night.

No, this would not stand. How could these other villages take Italian food and call it their own? "We may not like French food," Sergio pointed out, "but at least the French have enough self-respect to prepare just French food!"

Another Italian staff member snickered that the only reason French food is decent is because Catherine de' Médici brought her Italian cooks and showed the French how to eat properly.

"Yes, but she did become the queen of France, then," Sergio refuted, insinuating that Catherine was somehow a traitor to the Italian cause.

Peace was made with the French (for now), and they were even declared "Mediterranean cousins," by Sergio, who had earlier wanted da Vinci's masterpiece returned. The indignity paid by the Germans toward pizza and Nutella, however, could not continue.

Matteo decided to make a statement to the rest of the language camps that pizza is indeed Italian. Period. He devised a plan to make the "World's Largest Pizza" beginning with one fourteen-foot-long slice made of papier-mâché to bring to International Day, when all of the camps converge on the main square at the host village: the German camp. For the next four weeks, he worked for hours after others slept to make this giant replica and even led a workshop with campers to explain that Neapolitans invented pizza as a gift to Queen Margherita when she visited Naples in 1889. The classic pizza Margherita has the three colors of the Italian flag: green (basil), white (mozzarella), and red (tomatoes); each time you eat pizza, you are eating a bit of Italy.

Meanwhile, other Italian villagers practiced their soccer moves for the mini World Cup played at International Day between the different camps. Bonifacio, the team coach for the Italian camp, tried to keep the practices lighthearted and fun, wearing a beaming smile on his face. The campers, on the other hand, just wanted to win. The practices became so serious that half the players were limping the day before the big match. The goalie demanded his mother ship him an express package with his goalie gloves, hoping to improve the chances that a ball wouldn't slip through his fingers and cause a humiliating defeat.

The morning of the big day, the Italian staff and campers painted their faces green, white, and red to show their pride. To prevent a patriotic showdown of flag waving, I made a half-hearted announcement after breakfast that the idea of International Day is that we are all citizens of the world, not just of one (adopted) country. Italo, a precocious eight-year-old boy with glasses that constantly slipped down his nose, agreed amiably, "Just to be nice, I'm not going to bring up Hitler at the German camp."

The Italian camp's soccer team left early for International Day to participate in the quarterfinals. The rest of us loaded up the buses taking all the other campers to the German village. Matteo arrived exhausted after spending all night finishing his giant pizza creation. He had jettisoned the idea of having eight huge pieces come together to make one big pizza pie in the middle of the square. Even so, his one giant slice of pizza took six campers to triumphantly carry it to the bus. His arts-and-crafts handiwork didn't even come close to squeezing through the accordion doors of the bus. I suggested tying the pizza to the roof, but the wise driver wouldn't hear of it. He envisioned the newspaper headlines the next day screaming, "Motorist killed by giant flying pizza!"

We had to act quickly to avoid being late for the opening festivities. Rather than leave Matteo's artwork behind, we bent the crumpling papier-mâché pizza and jammed it through the rear door of the bus as the emergency alarm blared.

Fabio assured us, "This is OK because that's how we eat our pizza in Naples: folded."

The bus parked at the Norwegian camp, and another unforeseen difficulty presented itself: we had to walk a kilometer to the German camp carrying the heavy pizza. Matteo convinced groups of ten campers at a time to trade off hoisting his weighty work of art over their heads. Many times, the campers wanted to chuck the piece of pizza into the woods, but he spurred them on, saying that we needed to make a good impression, a *bella figura,* when we arrived.

The din of International Day rang through the trees. Music thumped, horns blared, and shouts of happy campers shook the forest. When the Italian villagers walked into the square with the giant slice of pizza over their heads, most people were too enthralled with dancing, chatting, and having fun to notice us newcomers. Those that did couldn't tell that what we were carrying was a pizza slice since it was raised above our heads and was bent.

The Italian soccer team greeted us with the results of the game, "Yes! We obliterated them!" They had handily won the first match against the Spanish camp, but some of the Italian players felt bad because the other team had kids eight years younger than they were. They took pity on the Spanish and to spare their feelings, scored only two goals.

The referee then announced that the final play-off game would be a "friendship match," and anyone could participate since the day wasn't long enough to have a complete tournament. This way we could all be winners. "Friendship?" asked the Italian goalie with his fancy gloves. "What do they mean? Friendship? What the hell is that? We want to win the world cup!" He sulked, but the Italian coach, Bonifacio, laughed heartily and encouraged them all to have a good time.

As the day came to a close and the Italian villagers gathered to walk back to our bus, I looked around for the giant piece of pizza, but it had been thoroughly trounced into little scraps of paper. The Roman counselor wasn't discouraged, though, and judged his statement a success. "Next year I'm going to make the Colosseum!"

ITALIANS AT A TYPICAL AMERICAN FESTIVAL

AT SEVEN, OUR SON WAS OLD ENOUGH TO ATTEND OVERNIGHT camp, so he chose his new camp name: Leo, short for his hero Leonardo da Vinci. I wrote his name on all his clothes—from his Batman cape to his Spiderman underwear—and Katy folded it all into an enormous suitcase double his size. Leo had already seen how Italian camp works, so I convinced him to attend the "rival" German camp as a spy to learn their tricks. Leo squirmed at the thought of leaving us, but when he looked at the enormous timber-and-plaster Bavarian buildings, he realized that compared to the bare-bones Italian camp, this was a luxury trip to Old World excess. He assured me that he took his covert mission into the enemy territory seriously and said he'd report back in Italian so the Germans wouldn't understand. Over time, though, I realized our little infiltrator was compromised—he fell in love with the German camp.

One of the Italian staff, Nina, from Torino, worked at the German camp when the Italian camp wasn't in session. She told me about the fantastic *tiramisù* cakes served at snack and the sweets shops open twice a day where the children could buy as much as they liked. (I had decided to open the Italian candy store only every other day and limit the amount campers can buy. The parents applauded my decision, but the kids weren't quite so happy.) Nina snuck out the details about the sugary climax of the parade of desserts: the decadent *Eisbombe,* a giant platter with a dozen scoops of ice cream covered with chocolate sauce and sprinkles.

"This is just like Pinocchio's *Paese dei Balocchi!*" Nina proclaimed, referencing Pinocchio's trip to the Land of Toys, where there was no school; kids played all day long and became donkeys. If the goal, though, was to learn German, this approach obviously worked. As they dug in with their spoons, the kids rattled off all sorts of Teutonic expressions of joy.

When we picked up seven-year-old Leo at the end of his two weeks at German camp, he informed me, "German camp has everything." Because of generous gifts from wealthy donors, the camp had a fleet of bicycles, a pottery kiln, a cinema, a giant floating iceberg for jumping off of, horses, a secret camping spot on the other side of the lake, a ropes course, archery, and even a speedboat. At the Italian camp we staged gladiator battles with armor and shields made out of cardboard and tinfoil, but at German camp the Teutonic knights fought with actual plate armor, helmets, and steel swords.

Our little spy—or perhaps double agent?—Leo revealed many of the wealthy camp's secrets. I already knew that the cooks served Nutella every morning, pizza from the wood-fire oven on special occasions, cappuccino at the café, and *tiramisù* for dessert. Now Leo disclosed they had Chinese takeout and performed Brazilian capoeira. He asked, "Chocolate croissants are German too, right?"

When he saw Katy, he ran to her with his arms open for a big hug. "I love you, Mamma!" he said and expressed how much he had missed us. "Now that I've survived here for two weeks, when

I get home, I can do whatever I want, right?" he asked. Then he remembered that we'd come to drag him away from camp, all his new friends, and all his newfound freedom. He slugged Katy in the arm and screamed, "I hate you!"

He tried to hide from us, but the German dean, Karl, took a break from greeting other parents to help us round him up. Leo was furious we dared shatter his perfect world but was asleep within five minutes for the four-hour car ride home.

We learned to make no demands on a child who had just come back from camp. Leo moped around singing camp songs to himself. We dug through his suitcase and discovered musty swimsuits, blackened socks, and, most disturbing, stacks of clothes that he never wore, meaning that he wore only a couple of outfits for two weeks. Katy determined which clothes to clean and which to burn.

Leo finally perked up when I showed him the camp schedule for the next summer. Suddenly he forgot his sorrows and imagined the next time and all the fun he'd have. I assumed he would repeat the same camps he'd attended this summer, but he announced, "Next year I'm going to Japanese camp!"

Even so, Leo was convinced we were punishing him by making him leave the German camp, and he took days to recover from the fun. He woke us up in the middle of the night to report on his terrible nightmare about the German dean: "What happens if Karl dies? There will be no more German camp!"

Karl was an imposing figure and had succeeded in converting the site from a rustic north-woods camp into a Bavarian paradise. He envisioned his village as reflecting a modern Germany beyond lederhosen and dirndls—an international European utopia. Katy had had enough of the cultural appropriation when she heard that

German camp had plans to build an Italian *gelateria* to make fresh gelato. "This has gone too far!" Katy proclaimed and demanded I talk to Karl. "The German camp is becoming Italian camp. They must at least have a German word for 'ice cream parlor'!"

I asked Karl about the scheduled new building with the new cinema and *gelateria.*

"Which building?" he replied. "We have eight new buildings planned."

Obviously, the Italian camp was the poor southern cousin. One of the little girls who visited the German camp after being at the Italian camp was shocked by the luxury. She told her friend, "Can you believe that they all have electricity in the cabins? Wow!"

I tried to keep up the spirits of the Italian staff by pointing out that our camp is in pristine wilderness on two lakes with a fabulous beach. We didn't have telephones and air conditioning in the cabins, but they were classic wooden cottages.

We didn't have washing machines at the Italian camp, as they did at the German site, so on the weekend break we took some of the older campers who were staying for a whole month to the nearby town of Hackensack to do laundry. Our visit coincided with the town's annual summer festival.

The Italians in their Dolce & Gabbana T-shirts and Versace sunglasses were easily visible amid the Minnesotans dressed in camouflage everything, T-shirts with slogans, and sweaty baseball hats. Fabio seemed satisfied, "These are the Americans I was waiting to see."

The female emcee put on an exaggerated southern accent. She looked at us through her pink, heart-shaped glasses—so she could "see the love!"—and announced the day's events. On the shore of the lake, several gutters were filled with water so fairgoers could bet on the minnow races. By the playground was a watermelon seed spitting contest, and near the picnic tables we could bet on the chickens. A numbered grid was laid out in the hens' cage, and participants bet on where the chickens would poop. In spite of my insistence that I'd never seen anything like this before, the Italians were impressed by this "typical American *festa.*"

A pilot of a Beaver model floatplane stood proudly on the beach, selling five-dollar raffle tickets for a free trip for a group of people in his plane. Lucio, a counselor who didn't know Italian but survived by mixing his Spanish and French, paid $20 for four tickets, calculating that this was not a crowd that would spring for such expensive tickets. When the pilot drew Lucio's name as the winning ticket, the event organizers seem somewhat annoyed that a local hadn't won. While we moved on to the next event, Lucio scheduled a time for the plane to land on the lake at camp.

We discovered the most popular area revolved around pies, or at least some sort of food in pie tins. A man and his wife signed up for the pie-throwing contest. The husband put on safety goggles and poked his balding head through a toilet seat mounted on a wall.

"You're not going to throw a pie at me, are ya?" he taunted. "Da wife," in her hot-pink floral-pattern dress, lobbed aluminum pie tins filled with whipped cream at his head but didn't come anywhere close to hitting him. The cream splattered in all directions, and the Italians meticulously looked over their designer clothes for errant pudding. "Missed me!" he jeered at his wife. She couldn't stand it and promptly jammed two pies right in his face. They laughed at the mess. The horrified Italians couldn't resist shooting photos to send to friends back home. A garden hose sprayed them both down.

This sight was rivaled only by the pie-eating contest, which once again had little to do with actual pies. An enormous woman challenged a relatively slight young man in John Lennon glasses to a duel, and the fight began. The "cooks" filled a dozen pie tins from a giant can of "chocolate-flavored custard." Neither of the contestants used utensils as they ate, and the pudding-like substance covered their faces and hands. The crowd chanted "Eat! Eat! Eat!" We left, a bit nauseated.

The next day, a group of German campers arrived at the Italian camp for a visit, and I knew I'd hear about all the decadent activities at German camp. One of the German campers got out of the van and asked me, "Dario, are you like the *Karl* of Italian camp?"

I thought a minute. "No, Karl is the *Dario* of German camp."

One of the German counselors, Alexandra, told me how tired they were because while we were at the festival, the Germans celebrated Oktoberfest with knockwurst, giant pretzels, authentic Bavarian mustard, and kegs of root beer. We also heard about the environmental program housed in the most eco-friendly building in the United States, which cost more than a million dollars.

Our staff was a bit glum when we heard about all the activities that the well-funded German camp could afford. Fabio tried to make the best of the sunny day and offered the fifteen German visitors a snack of cookies and water down by the beach during free time.

Just then, Lucio ran to the beach shouting, "The plane! The plane!" The Beaver floatplane splashed down and scooted up near the beach. "Our plane has arrived," he announced to the perplexed German counselors.

"The Italian camp has a plane?" Alexandra asked amazed.

"Of course," Lucio shrugged as Tiziana and several other counselors climbed aboard the plane for a ride. I stayed back, knowing my stomach wouldn't survive the trip.

The Beaver buzzed back to life and took them for several spins overhead as the campers waved from the beach. "Just wait until we tell our dean," Alexandra said, insinuating that the German camp would want to up the ante.

After the brief flight, the counselors stumbled out of the plane. Lucio was pale from motion sickness and got sick soon afterward. Even so, the Italian staff were happy to show the Germans how much fun a day at Italian camp can be.

BAT CAMP

EVEN THOUGH NORMA LIVED IN THE CENTER OF MILAN, SHE assured me that she loved the outdoors and would be a great counselor. Then she came to northern Minnesota. She was convinced bears, wolves, moose, coyotes, raccoons, and many other beasts couldn't wait to sink their teeth into her perfectly tanned Milanese flesh. I assured her that those animals are seldom dangerous to humans and in fact she should be more concerned about mosquitoes, ticks, and skunks. This didn't help. Now she added these creatures to her list of wild enemies that wanted to eat her, or at least make her smell bad.

She felt relieved when all the Italian staff and villagers packed up for an overnight at the luxurious German camp. Finally they would get a break from our more primitive camp, where drooling beasts of the forest preyed on ill-prepared Italians who don't know how to club bears or take down a wolf with a Swiss army knife.

That night in the German camp, most of the Italian villagers were going to have a big slumber party above the Gasthof dining hall in a beautiful room with high-vaulted, wooden ceilings. Girls would sleep on one side, and boys on the other with a line of counselors in the middle to prevent any secret midnight rendezvous. The counselors told me politely that if I, the dean, slept there, it might ruin the festive atmosphere. I thought about joining a group of boys in our environmental program who were going to sleep in the first certified PassivHaus in the United States, which produced all its own energy through solar and geothermal heating. Zeta told me that I should let the kids have a bonding experience without their dean around to spoil the fun. So, I slept on a couch in the building next to the infirmary while Zeta slept with the kids.

Sometime after midnight, a sixteen-year-old staff member who worked in the kitchen captured a bat she found next to her sleeping bag. She bravely cupped the drowsy bat in her bare hands, walked downstairs to the Gasthof exit, and let the little bat free into the night air.

Toward morning, Lucrezia woke up with a bat trying to nuzzle her in her sleeping bag. Groggy, she wondered what on earth this cuddly little creature was. She promptly threw her sleeping bag over the bat, where it was calmed by the darkness and warmth. She then carefully nabbed it in an ice cream bucket.

In the morning when I heard about the huggable bats, I passed on the news to Linda, the head nurse, who realized the seriousness of the situation. We called the Minnesota Department of Health, which told us that this incident was concerning because people had been sleeping. So we had to send the bat to be examined for rabies.

The campers didn't like that we had to ship the innocent bat to be killed and have its brain tested.

"Oh the poor little bat!" a camper said, remembering that the little guy had just wanted to cuddle with Lucrezia.

"Isn't there some way of taking its blood and letting the sweet thing go free?"

"Yeah! Bats are our friends!" said another who had learned this in her environmental lessons at the camp. "Bats eat mosquitoes, and the mosquitoes might have West Nile virus. The bats are actually doing us a favor!"

"How about we all make bat houses?" suggested a twelve-year-old camper. "Then we can have more bats and not so many mosquitoes."

The campers' sympathy for bats changed when I checked again with the head nurse, who now understood that the first bat had been let loose. The Department of Health informed us that if a bat had escaped from where people were sleeping, then everyone sleeping in the room had to get a rabies shot. I was shocked. We had to give shots to fifty kids?

I researched that the chances of getting rabies is less than .01 percent. First, the bat would have to want to bite us. Why would it? What are the chances of us not waking up if we have a bat on our skin chomping on us? The head nurse told me that it was possible we might not feel if a bat bit us because they have small, sharp teeth. Really?

I then reasoned that the bat would also have to be that one in ten thousand that had rabies, and no rabid bats had been found in our area. Linda said that even if the chance was miniscule, it was still there, and the disease is fatal. Symptoms might not appear for days, months, or years, but once symptoms appear, it is almost impossible to cure rabies. "Wait, I heard of someone who survived once," Zeta interrupted. "I guess he could barely talk afterwards, though, and was severely debilitated for the rest of his life."

In other words, we had to tell each parent.

The head nurse, Linda, assured us, "The good news is that rabies used to be a very painful shot in the stomach, but now it's just a series of five shots over a month."

"How can this be?" I asked. "That's 250 shots!"

Lucrezia pointed out that those five shots didn't include "the immunoglobulin, which is the one that goes in the backside." On an ordinary day, going into town from our remote site takes an entire afternoon. Now we had a logistical nightmare of hauling in dozens of kids every day for the next week or two.

Even though I wanted to stay, I figured that I'd be fired for this. I offered my resignation, but my boss told me, "No way! Now you have to step up and clean up this mess. Show us what you're worth." We started calling parents right away to tell them that if their son or daughter contracted rabies, they would die. The administration hoped to get ahead of the situation before any local media splashed this across the front page of the newspapers. We had to get permission for the campers to be treated at the local clinic and then recommend that they continue the regimen the next few weeks at home.

Parents' reaction to the news varied widely. Some parents from big cities were appalled that we hadn't eliminated all the bats from the area. However, one father from Minnesota dismissed the warning entirely, "There are bats everywhere, and they won't hurt us. My son slept in caves with the Boy Scouts, and nothing ever happened."

Zeta helped calm everyone down, and we let the kids call home to assure their parents that they were doing fine. I lent my cell phone to one of the campers, who told her dad, "Come to think of it, I did have a something nuzzling my hair last night. I just thought it was a big insect. I was so groggy that I didn't think much of it and pushed it away."

What? I thought when I overheard this. *Why didn't she tell anyone?* Now we had two bats unaccounted for.

My staff, however, were ready to mutiny. One brave counselor, Matteo, said he would play the odds because it was far more likely he'd be struck by lightning after winning the lottery. A buff young counselor from the East Coast broke down in tears and needed to lift weights to let off some steam. Norma felt vindicated in her belief that something in Minnesota would kill her. Rabies has been eradicated in Italy. "You Americans are so backward that this is still around!" she ranted.

Norma looked up rabies on the Internet. She returned to the staff later and announced that her doctor in Italy had told her she had to get a shot within twenty-four hours or she'd die. I explained that the Minnesota Department of Health usually took six days to test a bat for rabies and then would make a recommendation, so we had time. Besides, the local clinic had only two doses on hand, and the rest would be sent up from Minneapolis in the next couple of days.

Norma didn't believe me and warned the rest of the counselors, "You know we're all going to die, right?" She panicked and exclaimed she had to "tell the truth" to the rest of the camp. The head nurse and I had to control her hysteria before everyone freaked out.

She yelled in Italian at a staff meeting, "I don't care about anyone else!" I repeated her words in English so I was sure the rest of the staff understood. Suddenly, I felt like we had been thrown into Camus's *The Plague* as each person decided how they would react to the supposedly imminent disease. Norma decided that if she didn't flee this place, she would die. When we ignored her demands to call an ambulance for her, she convinced us to take her to the bus to Minneapolis so she could receive the rabies shots there.

I thought her absence would settle down the situation, but I could sense some of the other counselors were wondering whether they should make a break for it too. "We are all in this together," I told them, but that sounded too much like we were all going down with the *Titanic*.

"Dario, you weren't exposed like the rest of us," Lucrezia reminded me. I didn't want to seem petty, so I agreed and refrained from reminding them that they hadn't wanted me there with them.

I told the staff that if they couldn't be calm, they shouldn't be with the kids, who could become even more terrified. Fortunately, the campers weren't too worried, mostly because Zeta had to get the shots as well and brushed it off as not a big deal. Everyone trusted Zeta.

The campers started receiving the shots. Lucrezia told me that the girls wore their cutest underwear when they got the shot in the rear. Zeta bought fun bandages to put over their injection marks. To pass the nervous minutes in line for a shot, the campers sang Italian songs while the other, confused patients wondered if they were in the wrong waiting room. I knew that ice cream heals all tears, so we lined up at Dairy Queen before returning to camp.

One of the campers, Ala, called home to tell her little sister that she was now a vampire and she'd better look out. "When I come back, I'll be foaming at the mouth. You'd better give me my own room or I'm going to suck your blood."

The group of high school boys who had slept in the state-of-the-art, million-dollar environmental building away from the bats at first realized they could get lots of hugs from the cute girls if they were "reassuring." Some of the boys were a bit worried, though, that the girls might really be infected with rabies. Fortunately, they kept their distance.

Once the regimen of shots began, I tried to make light of the situation to cheer them up. My suggestion that this was a great chance to learn new Italian vocabulary was met with scowls. We projected the campy 1966 Adam West version of *Batman* in Italian with English subtitles. The students were used to the new terrifying versions of *The Dark Knight* and kept waiting for something wicked to happen. Halfway through the film, seventeen-year-old Franco stood up and shouted, "Wait a minute! This film is terrible!" Even so, a new camp song was born: "Na-na-na-na-na-na-na-na bat camp!"

The staff made a comeback too. Elisabetta printed *Squadra Pipistrelli!* (Bat Team!) T-shirts and dyed bowtie pasta black to make little bats to hang on the necklaces holding their name tags.

At the end of the week, the bat test came back negative, and we heard that if one of the bats in a colony has rabies, then the other ones likely do as well, so we could assume the colony was free of rabies. Those who panicked felt a bit silly after the fact, but no one dared say, "I told you so . . ." I never heard from Norma again, but Matteo said he heard that she made it back to Italy, vowing "never to return to those deadly forests."

BEWARE THE SHARKTOPUS AND SIDEHILL GOUGERS!

"Sidehill gougers" are fearsome creatures who make meals of slow-running campers, my counselors told me when I was six years old at YMCA Camp Christmas Tree. They assured us that we didn't need to worry about bears or wolves, just these other creatures that stalked the woods in search of fresh meat. We listened, gleefully panicked, as our counselor told us, "Your only defense is that sidehill gougers have one leg shorter than the other for walking sideways on steep slopes. Just run up or down the hill and they can't get you."

We loved the supposed danger, but we also did activities that today we don't do. We climbed (with no ropes) enormous dead elm trees, practiced archery, and shot BB guns (remember, I was six). We went happily on "swamp stomps" through nearby bogs, covering ourselves with sludge and thoroughly destroying our clothes. The finale was the two-foot-deep mud pit where we would get completely covered in filth before jumping in the lake.

As dean of an Italian language camp, I have to enforce safety restrictions that limit certain activities because "safety trumps everything," according to Linda, the health care authority for all the language camps. Despite all of the precautions, mishaps happen. Am I supposed to just keep the campers inside watching videos to prevent injuries? Atrophy would set in, and they'd all get fat and boring. I told the staff that I wanted a "new" Italian camp, where campers were active, in spite of the perceived dangers.

Neva and Alpina from Bergamo were more cautious. I noticed that they usually wrapped a scarf around their necks to avoid catching a cold, despite the scorching hot temperatures. Neva remembered the advice from her grandmother, "My nonna always said that you should never go swimming for three hours after eating."

"Three hours?" I replied. "But la nonna and la mamma are always pushing snacks, so essentially you'll never swim."

"Every year someone dies!" Neva added. "There's always an article in the newspaper that someone went swimming with a full stomach and never returned."

"Really?" I wondered.

"Yes! Eggplant parmesan is particularly dangerous because it's like a rock in your stomach. Remember: La nonna is never wrong!"

I ignored her cautious warnings and opened the beach. Strangely, Neva would often be one of the first swimming. She laughed, knowing full well she was living dangerously.

To promote a more active camp, I insisted on vigorous capture-the-flag matches, in spite of the possibility of some scraped knees. Bonifacio, who worked the first half of the summer for the French camp at our site, told us that they no longer did big capture-the-flag games but opted for more calm activities. He told us that the French used to play capture the flag throughout the entire camp including the woods. When I wanted to do the same, Letizia questioned my judgment, so I asked the nurse to bring her first-aid kit to the center of the game, just in case. To avoid injuries, I banned flip-flops, but kids still stubbed their toes and bumped into each other with astonishing frequency. The kids viewed the game as a life-or-death situation, and I suppose I did too. Sixteen-year-old Annina even broke the safety rules by wading chest deep in the water to sneak across the border to steal the flag. Another camper dressed up in a giant camouflage "Swamp Thing" outfit to protect his flag. He melded perfectly into the background and never moved the whole evening. His flag was never captured, so he declared victory, though he hadn't moved a muscle. Swift, eleven-year-old Leo almost grabbed the flag of the opposing team, but one older teenager clipped his legs as another tackled him. He caught his breath but then had the wind knocked out of him by another camper, Cinzia, who admitted, "I hate to lose, even if it's just a game. I have to win, otherwise it's no fun." Her team lost to Leo's, but she was pleased that she had put me in jail twice. At the end of the game, several kids had scrapes and bruises, but most had big smiles across their sweaty faces. The nurse wasn't pleased, but the kids raved that this was the best game ever.

To try to top capture the flag, the usually careful counselor Elisabetta planned a silly version of the famous horse race in Siena, the Palio, with mascots from each group dressed as a unicorn, a caterpillar, a she-wolf, a panther, and an owl. Elisabetta had cropped reddish hair, perfect posture, and a mischievous sense of humor, which she kept cautiously hidden, leading the other counselors to fear her. I expected a more controlled race from Elisabetta, but she ordered kids and counselors to hop on bicycles and gallop around the slippery soccer field. The fans watched from the middle, as they do in Siena, eager to witness the mayhem. "Well, at least they all have helmets, so this matches the ACA standards," she said. Despite bikes skidding around turns on the wet grass, incredibly, no one was injured.

Most injuries seemed to happen when we were *not* letting them do supposedly treacherous activities. Twice, kids started playing soccer in bare feet or flip-flops while waiting for the next activity and broke a foot. One camper set the record for the shortest time at camp without injury when he broke his ankle simply playing Frisbee shortly after his parents dropped him off. Some summers, we have had a camper limping along the dirt paths with crutches, but fortunately parents generally understand the risks.

If the nurse wasn't at the scene, the staff and kids always looked to me for safety procedures, so I took a lifeguarding class to have some legitimacy. I told the staff that all counselors must take the swim test to set an example for all the kids, who had to do the same. As with any rule, there were immediately exceptions: Elisabetta had asthma; Bonifacio, in spite of once being eligible for the Cameroonian national soccer team, had never learned to swim. The kids generally went along with my new requirement, but some worried me, such as plucky little Assunta, who assured us, "I'm really good at swimming; it's just I can't breathe."

Several of the native Italian female counselors came up with feeble excuses to avoid getting in the water, because they were "used to the blue Mediterranean" and terrified about what was lurking in the clean, but green water. It didn't help that Elisabetta taught us a melodic song about the carnivorous dragon in the lake, which translates something like this:

His eyes are red as blood,
His teeth are like knives.
Kids who step in the mud,
Will surely lose their lives!

Elisabetta sang with a smile about how the dragon would eat every part of your body and even feast on your cadaver at the funeral.

The usually tough, seventeen-year-old camper Franco wondered, "Elisabetta, you're not, like, going to kill us in our sleep or anything, right?"

The counselors Martina and Liliana then started a rumor that a vicious *squolpo,* or "sharktopus," was looking for a good meal of young kids. They prepared a "Risk of Sharktopus" meter and said that everyone needed to put on their anti-sharktopus cream (sunblock) to avoid certain death. The youngest campers were thrilled about this cryptozoological creature, and seven-year-old Leo reported to Martina, "I saw a *squolpo* off the dock!" He later recanted his testimony when precocious eight-year-old Italo, questioning this pseudoscience, pointed out that "neither sharks nor octopi live in freshwater lakes . . . Besides, how would they mate?" In spite of his scientific reasoning, Italo didn't dare enter the lake.

To prove to Italo and the others that the water was harmless, I sat in the shallow end of the swimming area with our three-year-old daughter, Stellina. One day, I noticed a yard-long shadow a couple of feet from the shore and assumed it was a thick tree branch floating just under the surface. With a splash, the branch came to life and splashed out into the deep. I caught a glance and noticed the jaws and fins of giant pike.

"Oh that's just a baby muskie coming in to get warm," Remo, an avid fisherman, informed me.

"A baby? It was three feet long!" I responded, nervous that it could have munched on little Stellina's toes.

"They won't hurt you. It's only the little sunfish that nibble," he pointed out. Perhaps after all it was good to have those lifeguards in six inches of water to scare off the killer muskies. It didn't help alleviate fears when the French waterfront manager from earlier in the summer showed the staff an X-ray of a three-inch nail sticking out of the heel of a poor camper who impaled her foot while just walking in the water. "It looks worse than it is," she said. "Statistically, we've been extremely lucky."

I'd been constantly calming down the staff about the dangers of the woods—bats, bees, and poison ivy—and laughing at the fake monsters in our midst. Perhaps I'd been wrong. Perhaps I'm more cautious now, but I'll always take the danger of the outdoors over the slow erosion of the mind and body when cooped up inside.

Then I heard that a tree pinned a camper at another camp while they were running for shelter. After hearing the story, little Italo remarked, "Trees are our friends, except when they fall on us."

KEEP 'EM SEPARATED

A MOTHER PULLED ME AND NINA ASIDE WHEN SHE DROPPED HER daughter off for two weeks of language camp. "Is someone with the kids at all times?" she desperately needed to know.

"Yes," I assured her. "Obviously there are times when they go to the bathroom or run up to the cabin to fetch something, but all the activities have counselors."

Finding my response unsatisfactory, the mother confided in Nina, her daughter's counselor, "I mean, my daughter is really beautiful, and the boys go crazy. Someone must be with her at all times!"—as if groups of boys would be waiting in the woods to pounce on her.

Nina promised the mother that she'd be extra attentive to her darling daughter. Afterward, Nina turned to me. "I'm sorry, but her kid isn't *that* beautiful!"

I was more concerned about the girls being boy crazy than vice versa. Tiziana's cabin group of thirteen- and fourteen-year-old girls primped and preened and applied too much makeup before the big dance party. They giggled and flirted with the gawky, clueless boys, who were annoyed by these girls with too much smelly perfume. The boys preferred to play Pokémon games and foosball.

Camp has a reputation of being a hot spot for summer loving, but the gossip is far worse than reality. Letizia reminded counselors at our staff meeting that when campers want to know about our personal lives, we must tell them, "I'm thirty-five years old, married, and have two kids: Marco and Sara."

Personally, I think living in such proximity often repels potential couples. For example, after two weeks of camp, Salvatore announced, "I'm never having children. Never." The buff waterfront manager, Giulio, complained, "Working at this camp is the best birth control there is." But Tiziana disagreed and soon wanted to have kids more than ever.

When the villagers arrived at camp, we searched their bags for "contraband," mostly cell phones, computers, books in English (which are confiscated for the session so they can concentrate on learning Italian), and food, so mice didn't join us in the cabins. Only once did we find condoms. Franco, a surly seventeen-year-old boy, brought them perhaps just to impress his cabinmates. In any case, both the nurse and I had a discussion with him about appropriate behavior at camp and what could get him sent home. Then we left him with the prophylactics because, as Letizia advised, "We need to keep track of all the campers because in the end, we want to send home as many campers as arrived. No more, no less."

We stayed especially watchful of the older kids, but at most the touching was handholding, and the girls wanting to sit in a ring and give back rubs. The oldest camper, Leonardo, refused to join the girls' circle and mocked them: "Welcome to Italian camp! Now turn around and massage your neighbor."

Little Giorgio replied, "That's nothing. At French camp they do facials!" In addition to learning about back-rub circles at some camps, I heard about "cuddle puddles," which were explained to me as "When someone is feeling down, everyone else snuggles up against them to make everyone feel part of the group."

I put my foot down: "Nope. No 'cuddle puddles' at Italian camp. We're not going there!" But one of the male Italian counselors was curious to learn more about "this American habit of 'the cuddle puddle.' This is very interesting!"

Shortly after, I was asked to accompany a bus full of French campers to the airport between sessions since the camps were short a chaperone. The director passed me a sheet with phone numbers in case of emergency and itemized the rules for the ride home. A bold warning listed the number one danger for chaperones to watch for as "cuddling under blankets" by couples. I didn't want to demand a humiliating "Hand check!" every fifteen minutes, and was relieved that the flyer explained that even with air conditioning, there's no reason to allow blankets!

Mostly, the kids just stared at their smartphones, a luxury they had been deprived of (and had forgotten). I was sad that all the friendships and goofiness could suddenly be eclipsed by these magical electronic devices. I remembered riding a rattling old school bus from camp and singing horribly out-of-tune ballads with all the other kids until we were hoarse. These kids had a luxurious coach bus with the latest Disney films on television screens throughout the bus. After two hours, though, the kids broke into loud French songs with goofy gestures, singing for the rest of the trip home, and I suddenly missed the quiet. This was the buildup to another long good-bye, the breakup of summer loving, when the bus reached its destination and the parents scooped up the kids, unwittingly crushing camp romances.

When I was back at Italian camp, I told the counselors to be extra attentive to the teenagers so they didn't sneak off into the woods. Sergio was the cabin counselor for the older boys and assured me that I didn't need to worry. He'd overheard a conversation late at night:

Tiberio asked his friend, "Leopoldo, have you ever had any sexual interactions?"

"Well, no," Leopoldo responded. "Unless you count my hand."

Besides inexperience, the other help we had in keeping the campers from touching each other was hygiene. Two fourteen-year-old boys forgot to bring their toothbrushes but failed to tell anyone or bother to buy new ones from the camp store. Somehow, they avoided the twice-daily group trip to the bathroom sinks and ignored their counselors' reminders that it was time to brush teeth. Instead, they didn't clean their teeth for an entire week. One of the mothers had to send her son to the dentist when he arrived home, but she blamed her son, "Fourteen-year-olds are just dippy! They have the body of an adult and the mind of a child."

A trip into the boys' cabins was often an olfactory assault, in spite of the counselors' best efforts. Apart from wet swimsuits not hung up to dry, we often found dirty underwear and socks caked on the floors, even after the campers left. Little Vittorio, who was just seven, sometimes peed his pants because "There's just so much funniness!" To make sure campers dealt with these issues, the nurse took a daily tour of the cabins and gave an award for the cleanest cabin. In other words, everyone knew the dirtiest cabin.

The littlest kids sometimes did their duty at night in pull-ups, or as they call them "just-in-case pants." I assumed that after a night pickling in their juices or following an hour of soccer with Bonifacio that the kids would want to jump in the shower. Many of them, though, seemed positively allergic to running water. At least I knew they would get somewhat clean from taking a sauna or a swim. I explained to them that water fights with squirt guns and water balloons didn't count as getting clean. Frequently the counselors had to insist that the campers hop in the shower and use soap. Even so, some kids didn't seem to understand this, such as eleven-year-old Samuele, who told his counselor, "Soap tastes good."

Every summer, there would be one kid who would only take a shower in his swim trunks. Even when the counselors tried to convince the campers they had nothing to be ashamed of, it was too late. Once a camper wore a swimsuit to the bathhouse, they all did the same. They didn't want to be the only one on display without clothes. Some kids even got dressed in their sleeping bags or hid in the tiny cubby/closet to put on their underwear. One night after dark, in a pitch black cabin, Samuele yelled, "Don't look at me! I'm naked." Of course all the other campers aimed their flashlight beams at him.

The first evening, the counselors would sit down with the new campers and hash out what new rules they should make so they could live together for two weeks. This empowered the kids to make their own regulations, and therefore they actually obeyed them. In one cabin, the counselors Fabio from Napoli and Matteo from Rome wrote down the comments from their younger kids in both English and Italian:

"No more nudeness!" shouted Marcolino, "and no touching my stuff!"

"No girls in the cabin!" Daniele demanded.

"Yeah, no hugging and kissing!" Alberto agreed.

"I don't want anyone jumping in my bed," Marcolino continued.

As much as the preteens are terrified of girls and boys, they are also obsessed with them. Nine-year-old Gian Marco dismissed all the girls at camp as nuts, saying, "Of course girls are crazy. They're going to be wommins someday!" At the same time, he was obsessed with the actress Megan Fox. One morning at a special weekend brunch, Luca, the head cook, served a big plate of bacon to each table, and Gian Marco loaded up. He envisioned a new superhero who would save the world: "Baconman! The best, most edible superhero!" Then he remembered his other obsession and reasoned that it would be great to have Megan Fox made entirely out of bacon. "Mmmm, 'Bacon Fox!'"

The young girls sensibly stayed away from these boys. Brunella, who was eleven, confided to her counselor, Gabriella, "I only like older men."

Gabriella hesitated, "Umm . . . what do you mean?"

"You know, like twelve and thirteen years old."

Most of the kids become fixated on the counselors and who might be seeing each other. I told the staff during our daily meeting that if I, as the dean, knew about the relationship, it was probably too public. I didn't mind couples forming and actually thought it was great if they found someone, but I didn't want these relationships to get in the way of their responsibilities. The campers already gossiped like crazy about the staff and presumed that all sorts of deliciously illicit incidents were happening just out of their sight.

One summer, two counselors, Francesco from Pavia and Angelina from America, fell in love and couldn't resist holding hands. They knew they should resist, but the two rival sides of camp—the boys and girls, the Capulets and Montagues—made the attraction of the star-crossed lovers overwhelming.

The villagers noticed, of course, and endless chatter erupted. Some of the female campers were jealous of Angelina because she had nabbed a cute boy. One evening right after dinner, we couldn't find Francesco and Angelina, who should have been hosting the evening *discoteca*. The villagers and even the staff were in an uproar, and rumors flew that the lovers must have found a vacant cabin. Lucrezia informed me, "Francesco and Angelina are missing and presumed indecent."

The couple turned up, not together, bearing supplies for the dance party, which was already in full swing and loud enough that Mr. Johnson on the other side of the lake had already threatened twice to call the sheriff. Angelina and Francesco's excuse fell on deaf ears. The campers giggled in delight, and the staff snickered. Angelina admitted to me that she regretted letting out any hint about the relationship's existence because now everyone assumed that any time they were not with the group, they were naked.

Once again, the talk was more fantasy than reality. Letizia reminded the staff that the best way to keep the campers out of our business was to stick to the same story. She repeated, "I'm thirty-five years old, married, and have two kids: Marco and Sara."

CUDDLY SKUNKS

"You're really roughing it now, honey! This is real camp-ing!" a mother told her daughter during opening day of Italian camp. I wasn't sure if this thrilled the girl or terrified her, but we weren't really roughing it, and this wasn't actually "camping." The cabins don't have electricity, but we sleep on fairly comfortable mattresses and have all our meals prepared by our head cook, Luca. Besides, the nearest town is just twenty minutes away.

Most kids aren't judgmental about where they will be staying for two weeks, but now because of her mother's reaction, Angioletta was a bit nervous. One mother confided, "I don't do nature," but she was pleased to have her son rough it so he would appreciate what he had back home.

Once the parents left, the kids would often breathe a sigh of relief; now they had some independence, which many had never experienced before. It didn't matter if they were from New York or New York Mills, what was important was making friends and having fun. My cool fifteen-year-old niece wore only the trendiest clothes to high school in St. Paul, but on her second day of camp she dressed up in a banana suit and sang a song about digesting, vomiting, and re-eating a banana. At camp, anything goes.

I've noticed that a window of opportunity opens up between about ages seven and nine, when most campers simply accept where they are and aren't stricken with homesickness. At camp, they can reshape who they are with a new name. They often have spending money for the first time in their lives. The surroundings seem much less important than everyone else's reactions to the surroundings. But if children wait until after ten years old to attend sleep-away camp, they often realize they are stuck at camp, and waves of nostalgia for home seep in.

I was surprised that the Italians generally loved the rustic site. We had no rugs, and Eva from Faenza declared that wall-to-wall carpeting should be banned. She especially couldn't understand why the German camp had carpeting in the dining hall. "How can this be sanitary?" she asked. "Just think of all the spilled food!" At our site, we had only rough wooden floors, walls, and ceilings. Of course this led to other concerns from the Italians, who were used to concrete and stone buildings back home. Some were worried we'd all die in a fiery inferno. "That could happen," I said, "so be careful. Isn't it a good thing we don't have electricity in the cabins?"

At camp, deer grazed in the soccer field early in the morning, and beavers swam along the shoreline, hauling freshly cut branches to their hideout. Nico almost bumped into a gentle fawn one evening on the way back from the bathroom. Eva stepped out of her cabin one morning to be surprised by a gray fox, who just stared at her, unafraid.

The parents were typically more nervous about nature than the kids, and some called our business office every day asking desperately for updates. We began to post photos on our website and uploaded little video clips of events, so the parents could keep an eye on their children from a distance. I was uncomfortable with the surveillance, but realized I enjoyed seeing photos of my kids when they were away at camp too. Then came the calls.

"Isabella doesn't look like she's engaging with all the other kids in the photos," one mother told me. "Can you see if she's OK?"

I checked with Isabella to make sure she was all right. "Of course I'm fine," Isabella said. "Why?"

I explained that her mother saw some photographs in which she looked rather sad.

"My mom's watching me? Creepy!"

I reported to the mother that the daughter said she was fine, and the mother responded, "Perhaps you could get some photos of her playing and being happy."

Despite this stream of images, we received bitter complaints when we skipped a day of photos due to a field trip. I pointed out that we were busy with the kids, but one of the parents said that then we should have even more photos. Some even suggested posting webcams around our site to provide a live feed of images to the parents' computers.

Kids generally accept that we don't allow cell phones or other electronic devices at camp since we want them to be active with their new friends out in nature. Still, some campers try to sneak in phones by handing us a dead cell phone to hold while they're at camp and hiding a working one in the bag. One parent even slipped a phone into her child's bag so they could talk at night. Fortunately, the battery always dies within a couple of days because there are no outlets in the cabins. One persistent parent was so worried about her daughter out in the woods that she sneaked onto our site while all the staff were with the kids in the dining hall and left comforting notes for her daughter on her pillow.

To make the kids comfortable with nature, we took them to the

soccer field after dark to see the stars. We listened to the loons cry-
ing in the night and assured them that they weren't wolves howling
to the moon. One evening I told them about an unusual gathering
of fifteen loons I had seen early that morning gathered near the isthmus. The next day, I noticed three loons in the same spot close to
the shore and whispered to a group of kids that they should observe
this serene scene. As they took photos of the black-and-white birds
just twenty feet away, one of the loons grabbed another around the
neck with its beak and shoved it under water. I was horrified at the
dominant loon's attempt to kill its rival as the kids watched. They
didn't want any of the pretty birds to die. After two minutes under-
water, the aggressive loon allowed its weaker competitor to surface
unscathed.

"Oh, nature isn't so friendly, is it?" little Angioletta said.

Still, even the staff can hardly resist some of these cute little creatures. I heard about baby skunks living up near the German camp.
One of the maintenance crew found one of them caught in a live
trap early one morning and confessed to me, "I'm an animal lover,
so I had to let it go back to its mother."

When Alpina from Bergamo saw a skunk racing across the path,
she ran after the adorable fur ball to snap a photo. I yelled for her to
stay back, because if she got sprayed, she'd have to bathe in tomato
juice for a week to get rid of the smell.

"You Americans are strange," Alpina responded. "You need to
eat tomatoes, not take a bath in them!" Luckily, she couldn't find
the skunk.

Late one evening as we finished our evening program down at
the beach, we watched dark clouds threaten in the distance, and
violent thunder echoed across the lake. A couple of nervous campers admitted they were scared of storms. I told them that I love the

lightning and the fresh air that the electric show brings. I pointed out that the storms scare off the oppressive heat and humidity, but my words were drowned out by a thunderclap, and we ran to our cabins to beat the impending downpour.

The kids want to tame nature, but mostly they want the wilderness to leave them alone. The day after the thunderstorm, when the humidity (and bugs) returned, I heard a camper slam the screen door and run outside while yelling, "A spider! A spider!" He ran for his life as his cabinmates grabbed their cans of Off! and prepared for battle. In the nick of time, the counselor halted them before they filled the cabin with bug spray or sprayed haphazardly into each other's faces. We usually make the campers leave their aerosol bottles just outside the screen door, otherwise they would soak the cabin with the insecticide. I explained that spiders (along with dragonflies and bats) eat mosquitoes. I didn't dare ask them who made all the cobwebs in the eaves of the cabin, or no one would sleep at night.

Italo used up his entire spray can of Cutter repellent in a week, and I worried that this might make him sick. I explained that the head of the YMCA in Minneapolis had shown me how he built up immunity to mosquitoes by just letting them bite him. He would never scratch the bites since it only makes it worse. "But that's crazy!" Italo yelled. "Who could withstand the pain?" After the campers scratched their bug bites to the point of bleeding, we took them to the sauna at the water's edge. The red hot blaze of the burning oak in the iron stove opened their pores and made their skin stop itching. They jumped in the lake at sundown to cool down, and I knew that they would fall fast asleep afterward despite the next thunderstorm that would strike that night.

THE CHEESE WIZ EATS CROW

ONE COLD JANUARY DAY IN THE DEPTHS OF A MINNESOTA winter—about as far as possible from a Minnesota summer day at camp—I received a phone call from a professor who asked rather cryptically, "What do you know about mascarpone?" He gave me the phone number of a cheese factory two hours away in Wisconsin that needed a translator for a group of Italians who would be setting up a two-million-dollar mascarpone plant. Since I needed work while I wasn't running the Italian camp, I signed up. I hoped to find some native Italian speakers who could work as counselors, and maybe the cheese factory would even donate extra Italian cheese to the camp kitchen.

At this point, all I knew about mascarpone was that it was Italian thickened cream and delicious in desserts such as *tiramisù*. Apparently, I knew far more than most of the cheese makers, who had never heard of mascarpone and massacred its pronunciation.

I was assigned to translate for the two Italian cheese consultants, who disdained each other's skills but were forced to work together. One of the Wisconsin cheese makers called them "Laurel and Hardy lookalikes" since Luciano is a goofy beanpole and Roberto is much shorter, stocky, and serious. Luciano was just twenty-eight years old and looking for love, though he was engaged to be married the following year. He blasphemed like a pro, and Roberto shook his head at Luciano's salty swearwords. His father was a well-known Italian cheese master who didn't like to fly, so he sent his son instead. The other Italians knew this, so they constantly teased and misled poor Luciano, who liked being the center of attention even if they were making fun of him.

The real cheese wizard, Roberto, was in his sixties but could work fourteen-hour shifts without sitting down and without taking a break to eat. His only interest was producing cheese, and he didn't talk about much else. He confused everyone by refusing to eat the cheese, tasting only a minuscule sample to check on the process. Even more baffling to Luciano was Roberto's refusal to smoke cigarettes, drink liquor, or do anything that Luciano considered "fun."

"Roberto is not Italian," Luciano concluded.

Regardless, Roberto's cheese credentials were impeccable. He had developed the first mechanized mozzarella machines, essentially making these fresh cheese balls in water available to everyone in Italy and then the world.

The two of them had recently returned from Siberia, where they had set up a factory. Roberto told me how restaurants there refused to serve water and offered only strong tea or vodka. Luciano, determined to keep up with his Russian hosts, finished his whole bottle of vodka. Roberto worked alone the next day as Luciano recovered.

Roberto and Luciano were brought on the Wisconsin project late and didn't approve of how the system was set up. Roberto scoffed at the evaporator, which was constructed for reducing the liquid in fruit juices, not milk. Still, the duo worked with the lead American manager of the mascarpone room, who had never even tasted this kind of cheese before. The semiretired boss of the plant rarely moved from his jumbo office chair, perhaps because he had tasted so much cheese during his career. He drove a king-sized Cadillac, swore in every sentence, smoked cigars wherever he damned well pleased, and welcomed the Italians with open arms. Luciano adored him and declared that "the big boss" was the true American that he'd always dreamed of.

While the boss did whatever suited his fancy, we had to dress in lab coats, safety glasses, and hairnets—even "beard nets" for the few Harley guys. We plugged our ears with industrial orange ear plugs, which made translating next to impossible when the machines thumped, bumped, and whirred. Roberto used many gestures to communicate over the noise. He waved frantically to the controller in the booth to "get over here" when dozens of gallons of milk splashed on the concrete floor, but the Italian gesture looked more like a greeting than a demand to "come here." The relaxed Wisconsinite just waved back, happy that the Italians were so friendly.

After eleven-hour days amid clamoring pumps, I was still on duty and supposed to make sure Roberto and Luciano got a good dinner since Roberto didn't take a lunch break. As we took off our lab coats in the office, Roberto blew kisses to Danielle, the rotund receptionist, who let him flirt even though he was a good thirty years older. Roberto told the other secretary, "You are beautiful too, but Danielle is my true love." He leaned closer to Danielle and whispered suggestively, "Soon it's spring. Do you want to go find Easter eggs with me?" I translated, and she looked at me to see if this was truly what he had said.

Luciano laughed at Roberto, pleased that he was loosening up. Luciano considered going out with Roberto and me that evening because the night before he had gone out with the workers from

Wisconsin and was almost beaten up. An inebriated Wisconsinite thought Luciano was making fun of him when he spoke the few phrases he knew in English in his thick Italian accent. Just like Jim the slave in *Huckleberry Finn,* the drunkard had never met a foreigner or anyone who didn't speak English.

The only place open past seven o'clock in Turtle Lake is a casino, but Roberto said he didn't have a tuxedo. I assured him that American casinos are very different from Italian ones and let in visitors who are not in black tie. In fact, the cheese plant manager told us excitedly that it was "Hot Dog Nite" at the casino, where we could buy as many hot dogs as we wanted for ten cents each.

Roberto was confused. "Now why would I want a hot dog?"

We noticed that all the calendars in the office had Saturday's "steak night at the casino" circled in blaze-orange highlighter. "I wouldn't miss that for the world: all you can eat steak!" the manager said.

"How much steak can you actually eat at one time?" Roberto asked rhetorically.

The manager nodded his head in delight and said that he skips all the side dishes and usually eats a good three pounds worth.

Roberto and I entered the casino, which had no windows, no clocks, plenty of smoke, and constant video surveillance. The wife of one of the cheese makers said that some gamblers stay for two or three days straight without ever leaving. When the casino opened some years ago, the richest man in the county began to gamble and was a pauper within a year.

Roberto wanted a light dinner of chicken, but the waitress brought him an entire chicken. "How on earth can I eat this?" he asked the waitress.

She explained that most people are excited about getting

so much food. "Besides you can bring home the leftovers for tomorrow."

This insult would not stand. Roberto whispered to me, "Do I look like the kind of person who takes food out of restaurants?" He refused to leave a tip. I slipped a tip on the table so we'd still be served the next evening. He noticed the cash and shook his head, "It splits my heart in two to do that."

Roberto and Luciano's efforts paid off as the Wisconsin mascarpone won blue ribbons as the best mascarpone in the country, beating even the Italian brands. Even so, the Wisconsin cheese maker couldn't sell enough of it at the beginning to make the whole operation worthwhile. Roberto was disgusted and had me translate, "Just let me bring a couple of Neapolitans over, and even if they don't speak English, I guarantee you that they'll sell your mascarpone." The Wisconsinites were a bit disturbed, thinking that this small Italian man perhaps wanted to bring the Mafia into the cheese business.

Roberto flew back to Italy since he had to travel to Siberia, Poland, and Sicily to set up more cheese factories, but he agreed to come to Italian camp to show kids how to make fresh Italian cheeses. Fortunately for us, the cheese factory donated a large batch of the extra mascarpone to our summer camp.

Our camp cook, Luca, made creamy sauces, created inventive desserts, and generally fattened up the food with this award-winning cheese. I hoped that this rich cream would soothe tensions among the staff at camp, who by the third week were tired, grouchy, and distracted. I had to ask one of the senior staff, Liliana, not to carry her e-reader around with her since none of the kids or counselors had phones or computers with them. She generally worked hard without any need for oversight, and she was stunned that I questioned her judgment. She claimed she was reading books on her tablet in Italian, which made it no different from an actual paperback. When I held firm, she fumed.

The next day, Liliana confronted me and said we had a serious problem. As I worried that she was going to quit, she argued, "Do you realize that *tiramisù* isn't even on the menu?" She had noticed the twenty-five pounds of mascarpone in the refrigerator and thought it was being "wasted" on other recipes and should be used for this delicious dessert. She demanded I go speak with Luca immediately.

I countered that Luca was making other great sweets and dishes with the cheese. I tried to change the subject and asked if she wanted to throw a big Italian wedding with a long *tavolata* set up with picnic tables outside. The wedding could involve our language hero, "Super Italiana," and Paul Bunyan and lots of feuding relatives. Gaetano wanted to be the pistol-toting priest marrying the bizarre pair. We could even bring in Romeo and Juliet with mock melodrama and jealous ex-lovers.

"Sure, that's all fine, but what are we going to do about the *tiramisù*? Don't you understand? This matters!"

Fortunately, Roberto, the cheese master, agreed to visit camp with his wife and teach the kids how to make their own mascarpone—Liliana was relieved that we would have plenty of it for *tiramisù*.

While waiting for the Italian desserts to arrive, I treated the staff to our annual trip to Dairy Queen on our day off. The camp business manager, Gianni, who is a ringer for Paul Bunyan and stands nearly double the height of some of the campers, wanted to make the most of free ice cream. "Last year, right after I ordered the large Blizzard, the nurse told me that DQ sold a super-secret thirty-two-ounce Blizzard, if you asked," he said. "I've been waiting for this moment all year." He asked the young girl taking orders if they had anything larger than the twenty-one-ounce Blizzard. There wasn't one listed, but they agreed to give him a thirty-two-ounce extra-large blizzard and an additional twelve-ounce one with the leftover ice cream. I calculated that the calories clocked in at almost 2,800. The native Italian staff, who ordered mini, twelve-ounce portions, shot photos of him consuming it easily.

The Italians generally scoffed at this decadent American food, at least until they tried it. Some were disgusted by ranch dressing on salad but often couldn't get enough of it once they tasted it. They laughed at the giant sizes of ice cream cones but took any chance to order one. Having raised the bar for what constitutes "supersized," Gianni mentioned a milk-drinking contest.

"These never end well," I insisted in an attempt to stop the excess.

Letizia, who is usually the voice of reason, told us that these weren't so bad. She recalled that her boyfriend Brad took the "gallon challenge" to drink a gallon of milk and had it all calculated out how much he could hold down in a set amount of time. Then she remembered, "He lost it all before the end, though."

As Gianni digested his giant ice cream dessert, he told us how he was the only one of his friends who could drink an entire gallon of milk. "I tried to make myself throw it up, but I couldn't. Instead I just sat around with that gallon of milk sloshing around in my belly all night." He patted his stomach, which was now filled with more calories than a normal person would need in a week.

I was always hesitant to talk with Luca, the cook, about the menu because chefs never seem to take criticism well. In fact, the cook before Luca had wanted to prepare *prosciutto e melone* with ham and watermelon rather than cantaloupe. When we refused to eat the soggy pork mess, he huffed and puffed that we were all snobs that couldn't be flexible.

Luca is generally good natured, but I chose my moments carefully to speak with him because I knew the camp's next meal depended on him. At first, Luca was exceptionally open to suggestions of Italian dishes to cook. I always passed the preliminary menu to the native Italian staff during orientation, who of course had dozens of suggestions. They provided their favorite recipe and were chagrined when Luca didn't include it.

Silvia, a dark-haired Italian from Cremona, took me aside and told me gravely, "Have you talked to the head cook about making lasagne? Lasagne are very important, you know." Luca assured them that he'd try to include their suggestions, but said that there are twenty regions in Italy with very different culinary traditions. We looked through his cookbooks and discovered *coglioni di mulo* (mule balls), rotund, wrinkly sausages from Umbria that are shaped like what their name describes, and a dessert of ricotta and chocolate named *le palle del nonno fritte* (fried grandpa's testicles). Somehow these didn't seem particularly camp friendly. When Luca served *linguine alla puttanesca* (linguine with the "whore's sauce"), Sergio couldn't wait to explain the dish's raunchy name to all the preteen campers and to note that the side dish of *piselli*, peas, is also slang for "penis." Letizia anticipated Sergio's intentions and succeeded in obstructing his off-color digression.

Because of the rash of food allergies and preferences, Luca had to make several different dishes each evening to satisfy not just the vegetarians and the vegans but the lacto-ovo-pesco-pollo-etc.-intolerant as well. Eight-year-old Elena confessed, "I'm allergic to gluten. It's my nemesis." Many kids and staff were simply trying out new diets, and Luca had to meet their requests whether he liked it or not.

Many of the native Italians didn't understand "this American obsession with allergies" and pushed the kids to try new foods. Nina was on a mission to make the delicious cornmeal polenta a favorite and taught the song "La Bella Polenta" about the process of growing, cooking, and eating this northern Italian staple. The kids revolted and dubbed it the "*brutta*," or ugly, polenta, and even Tiziana complained at how "ungodly long" the song was. Nina persisted, "I don't care. They're going to learn the song anyway!" When Luca mixed in gorgonzola, many campers declared polenta one of their favorite dishes, while others rebelled against it.

To foster the kids' connection to the earth, Alceste from Le Marche wanted the kids to plant a garden. Danielle, who was fourteen and couldn't stop eating, dutifully watered the seedlings in hopes of a feast. Then he searched in his dictionary for what exactly they had planted: "*Melanzana* is eggplant, not melons? That's what I've been watering all these weeks? I hate eggplant!"

Eva from Faenza was horrified at how American kids eat, so she helped them with table etiquette. She asked the girls at her table to pass the pasta around to everyone and say "*Buon appetito*" before eating rather than just digging in as soon as the food arrived. One evening, a colleague of mine from the university and her child sat at Eva's table. The little boy chopped his spaghetti into little bits rather than twirling the strands around the tines of his fork as we'd taught all the campers to do. Eva cringed but held her tongue since the mother was right there watching proudly. The mother didn't say a thing when the boy set down his utensil and shoved the pasta into his mouth with his hands.

Many of the kids just loaded up on massive amounts of carbohydrates. Others were pushed into new experiences. Campers sampled spinach and broccoli and discovered the smooth delight of *panna cotta*. Some survived on bread, bananas, and chocolate for the first few days but eventually relented when constipation set in. I remembered my brother's experience as a counselor on ten-day river trips in northern Wisconsin with painfully plugged up campers. He'd sneak a little dish soap in the dinner, and all their problems would be solved. Our nurse wouldn't let us use this cure-all.

Luca announced that he would serve American brunch on Sunday mornings. "What is this 'brunch'?" Michele asked me. When I explained it's part BR-eakfast and part l-UNCH, he was impressed. "You add an extra meal between breakfast and lunch?" he exclaimed. "We should import this idea to Italy . . . but then we would be as fat as you Americans."

Most campers loved the Italian food, though, and practically bathed in Nutella for breakfast. They wrote a song about Nutella. Leo once showed me his hands covered in the chocolaty spread and suggested, "I should put some Nutella under my fingernails in case I get hungry later."

To make the camp truly Italian, Sergio and another counselor asked for horse steaks. Luca said he'd be willing to cook these, but this was probably illegal. Instead, he suggested, he would serve roasted rabbit. "But don't tell the children it's 'bunny' or 'Thumper,'" he pleaded. "They did that at German camp, and none of the kids touched it."

Sergio didn't think that rabbits were challenging enough. "You need to cook cats because it's culturally authentic of the north, especially Vicenza," he said.

Luca just stared at him as I asked Sergio if he'd heard the recent reports about Saint Bernards, who come from near his town in the far north of Italy. "I've heard the Chinese are breeding them to eat since they can get so much meat," I told him.

"That's just wrong," he replied, as if eating cats was much healthier.

Bonifacio shook his head at our discussion and pushed us a step further. "I like bush meat," he proclaimed.

"What's 'bush meat'?" I asked.

"You know, all the animals you catch out in the bush: squirrels, elephants, lions."

"You've eaten a lion?" I asked. "Is that even legal?"

"Oh, I don't think it's legal, but my neighbor killed one in Cameroon when I was about ten, and we ate it."

"And elephants?" I wondered.

"I haven't eaten elephant, actually," Bonifacio clarified a little embarrassed, "but gazelle is my favorite. It's the best!" Bonifacio talked about the different snakes he'd eaten—"vipers and boa constrictors"—and how monkey is a bit like pork because of the texture of the meat. "The animals I don't like to eat are giraffes; they taste terrible."

I asked when he goes to the zoo if it's a big buffet. He just laughed.

The next day, Liliana wrote the "question of the day" on the white board in Italian for the kids to learn: "*Qual'è il tuo animale preferito*" (What's your favorite animal?). Bonifacio thought for a minute, "Do you mean to eat?"

"No!" Liliana replied. "Why would you ever think it would be to eat?"

Most of the time, Luca was remarkably patient and resilient in the face of these bizarre requests for food that he knew the kids would hate. He wisely ignored most of them. I thought him very brave to dare to cook Italian food for Italians when he'd never been to the country.

Then Roberto, the cheese master, arrived to make fresh ricotta and mozzarella for the kids. Roberto was unsatisfied with the risotto and not afraid to say so. Many people think a discerning palate is a sign of high class, but his saying, "In Italy, we would feed this rice to the hens" in front of one of the cooks didn't make him any friends. In fact, the rest of the kitchen staff were now terrified of the cheese wiz.

Roberto gave Luca plenty of advice on how to make better risotto. He explained that one trick is to take "large hunks of pig fat" and boil it into the rice so that white chunks remain at the end. He kissed the tips of his fingers and opened his hand to show how truly "*Delizioso!*" this is. Then Roberto advised getting a rifle to shoot all the crows around camp to make *risotto al corvo*.

"What are you talking about?" demanded Carlo, the pizza oven maker from southern Italy, who couldn't believe Roberto, the northerner, eats "crow rice."

Roberto insisted that it was the best possible rice.

"Don't crows eat roadkill?" I pointed out. "They're probably full of disease."

The cheese master ignored me and explained the recipe, as if we'd run home and prepare it: "First you shoot a crow. Then you pluck it, boil it, and chop the meat into little bits. Boil the bones in water for a nice broth for the rice. It's my favorite risotto!"

Carlo, still in shock, turned to Bonifacio. "Here's something I'm sure you've never had: crow!"

Bonifacio thought a minute, "Yes, I've had crow a couple of times in northern Italy. It's delicious."

Luca squashed the speculation about eating the scavenging birds, saying, "It's illegal to shoot crows in Minnesota," which I was sure he didn't know for sure. Thankfully, Luca stayed with more conservative Italian dishes. After he served the next lunch, he peered into the dining hall to see how everyone liked the *spaghetti alla carbonara*. Carlo saw Luca and grabbed him forcefully by the shoulders. He gave him a kiss on both cheeks and warned, "If you change anything with the recipe, I will kill you! You are a master of the *carbonara*." Luca appreciated the compliment but now wasn't sure if he needed to fear for his life or if Carlo was joking.

The campers ate massive amounts of the perfect pasta, but some went to waste. Another Italian, Nina, confronted Luca, "We had too much *spaghetti alla carbonara* at lunch and don't want it to go to waste." Luca took a note to cut down on portions for the next time.

Another Italian, Moreno, interrupted, "But please don't give us less spaghetti!" Luca tore up the note and resolved to just stop listening to the Italians.

That's why I was surprised that Luca let a Neapolitan and a northern Italian, Fabio and Nico, help him make spaghetti one evening. Dinner was put on hold as Luca accidently tipped twenty pounds of boiling spaghetti all over the linoleum floor. No more Italians in the kitchen.

By the second to last week, patience was wearing thin in the kitchen, and I warned the counselors to avoid giving any advice and stick to compliments if they wanted to eat well. Still, the staff couldn't help asking for more Nutella and begging, please, for *tiramisù*.

Luca snapped. All the kitchen staff fled the kitchen when he yelled at his assistant cook, "Get the hell out of my kitchen!"

I considered my options for supplying everyone with dinner

that evening. The cheese Roberto had made would just be a little snack. Carlo hadn't finished building the pizza oven, and ordering pizzas for seventy people from a bad pizzeria twenty miles away wasn't too promising. By the time I realized we were stumped, Luca had apologized to his cooking staff.

Perhaps to mend relations, Luca made a fantastic feast and topped it off with giant portions of *tiramisù*.

"*Sìììììì!* Hurrah!" Liliana and some of the kids screamed, as if the latest boy band had landed in northern Minnesota. Many of the campers had never heard of *tiramisù* but gathered that this had to be something special by the behavior of the counselors running up and down the aisles. The cooks realized that Roberto wasn't so bad after all if he could concoct such delicious mascarpone.

Each of us admired the jumbo serving of this creamy, caffeinated, chocolaty bit of heaven. Roberto didn't touch it, of course, but the rest of the staff indulged in this long-awaited moment. The concentrated milk fat seeped into our stomach, and the lipids into our veins. Even Gianni seemed to have eaten enough, for the moment. Many gripped their stomach in agonizing sugar-fueled bliss from overeating—near-death by chocolate. They wanted to be happy but patted their bellies in pain. Luca looked out from the kitchen with a satisfied smirk.

GOING *SAUVAGE*

At Italian camp, kids and staff assumed a new identity. We even had a list of names in Italian so they could leave their old selves behind. Letizia wanted to have enough names to avoid the confusion of having two kids with the same names, so the counselor Gaetano made a list of bizarre antiquated names. One girl stumbled on the name "Torquata," which the Italians said had been used only in the masculine by Torquato Tasso, a sixteenth-century poet. Gaetano poured on the charm and exclaimed that it was "*molto bello.*" She was hooked.

At the end of her two weeks at camp, her cabinmates, with ordinary Italian names such as Chiara and Maria, asked her why she chose such a strange name. "You mean I had a choice?"

To exchange her Euros for dollars from the camp bank, Torquata needed to sign her real American name. She signed her real first name, then hesitated. She asked herself out loud, "Now, what is my last name? What is my last name?" Gianni, the camp business manager, thought she was joking—she had shed her old identity only two weeks ago. When he realized she was truly stuck, he reminded her of her full name. "Oh yeah! That sounds right."

Campers also assumed that the counselors' personas at camp

were who they truly were. Eleven-year-old Romano assumed that the staff worked there year-round and asked us if we had been born there too. Then he stopped himself, realizing this was a silly question, "No, I suppose you were born in a hospital nearby. But have you lived here your whole life?"

Many of the new personalities were primordial versions of ourselves. The Norwegian camp let campers carry around sticks, and what could be better for a nine-year-old? But if a little boy has a big stick, doesn't he want to use it? Our son, Leo, wanted to do the same thing at Italian camp, but Nina said he could carry it around the trails but had to leave his stick outside the dining hall while we ate.

He refused because the stick had become part of his identity.

Katy, my wife, stepped in for Nina and told Leo that none of the other kids bring big ol' tree branches to dinner, so he should just leave it at the door and pick it up when he left.

"Do you know how hard it is to find a stick like that?" Leo rebutted. "Everyone wants one like that, and the minute I leave it, someone will snatch it."

Katy said that Minnesota is the "land of ten thousands sticks," but he wasn't buying it. Leo ran off to his cabin. Halfway through dinner, he returned to the dining hall, having stashed his stick safely somewhere far from all the other stick hunters and stealers.

The next day, I told him that I didn't want the stick situation to happen again.

"Exactly! I can't believe they wouldn't let me bring in my stick." Somehow, he convinced Nina to let him bring in his smaller stick (apparently his magic wand), which he banged on the table in delight. The poor counselors had to teach him that with a good stick comes great responsibility. Soon, many of the other little boys wanted big sticks too.

The power of the group pushed hesitant kids. A nervous group of teenaged girls ventured into the sauna for the first time on a dare. I was their lifeguard when they jumped into the lake, as the sunset shimmered purple ripples across the waves. One of them giggled, "That was the most disgusting fun thing I've ever done. We just sit here and sweat together and then jump in a cold lake in the dark. I love it!"

I avoided telling them that a garter snake sometimes sneaked through the floorboards during the day in search of warmth. Another gaggle of girls came into the sauna later and saw the snake. They screamed in terror and just about knocked each other over getting out the door. Brunella from Brainerd picked up the snake right under its head and brought it outside to show the others. "It's just a little garter snake. What's the big deal?" The other girls stopped screaming and went to take a look at the evil serpent squiggling. With their hearts pounding, they stepped back into the sauna to sweat out the adrenaline.

The next night, a cabin of little girls couldn't get to sleep because one of them found a spider. Then seven-year-old Emma told the frightened girl, "Is this the first time you noticed the spiders? They're everywhere!' she exclaimed. "During the day, they crawl up your legs. There are thousands of them up in the ceiling that come dangling down at night." As if fearsome spiders would descend right into their mouths and ears and suck out their brains while they slept. The little girls didn't sleep so well that night.

Slowly, though, most everyone got used to the little creatures in our midst. One of the assistant cooks didn't seem particularly disturbed when she was relaxing on the couch and felt something wiggle under her legs. A little chipmunk, "George," popped out and ran across the floor. She told me that earlier in the summer the

French head cook had tried to capture George's cousin in the dining hall and take him far away. He cornered it and slammed down a five-gallon bucket over it. Instead, the rim of the bucket popped off the poor creature's little head.

Our head cook, Luca, also unintentionally bumped off a mouse by leaving a bag of powdered sugar in the pantry. When he went to use the sugar for a birthday cake, he found the rodent had burrowed into the bag and had kept eating until it was so fat it couldn't move. "Now that's death by sugar!"

When a man came to tune the old piano in the lodge, he discovered why the keys in the second highest octave made odd sounds whenever played: a mother red squirrel had decided to raise her baby kits in a comfortable nest next to the strings. When we tried to drive into town to get some supplies to keep the animals at bay, the camp car had unusual electrical problems. The mechanic in town deduced that squirrels had eaten through the electrical lines. "Oh, we see that all the time. The wires must be sweet or something."

I tried to keep the staff calm about the tenacity of these rodents and hide that I was disturbed. The nurse heard mice in her cabin at night, so she moved into her car late at night. When she heard about the squirrels eating the wires, she pitched a tent outside her cottage. I suggested that perhaps kids had brought food into the clinic, but I realized it didn't matter. In my cabin, a mouse chewed right through my tube of Colgate to get to the goodness inside— apparently toothpaste is food. I had my comeuppance, however, when I discovered the hungry mouse drowned in my toilet. Even when the kids are initially afraid of these little creatures, we avoid telling them of their untimely deaths.

One cabin of the youngest girls was terrified because they had a mouse that was attracted by the chocolate Giulietta had brought into the cabin. The counselor, Irene, found the mouse on her bed, and Tiziana said, "She screamed so loud we thought she got murdered." Even so, Irene made the best of the situation to avoid panicking the kids. She explained that they had a visitor, a cute little mouse they named "Ivan." They had a little welcoming party for their mouse, but the festivities were cut short when Sergio announced triumphantly that he had caught little Ivan in one of his traps. The party turned into a funeral, and the girls cried for their lost friend.

Sometimes camp stinks—literally—or more correctly you can sometimes smell people coming. One year, Martina, Letizia, and many of the staff made a vow not to use shampoo the whole summer "to rejuvenate the natural oils" of their hair. Fortunately, they swam or took a sauna most days.

I also heard that the kitchen staff, mostly women who had worked the first half of the summer at French camp, had decided to go "*sauvage*" (wild) and have a contest to see who could urinate in the most bizarre places without getting caught. Fortunately, I found out about these pranks long after camp was over. One of them peed outside her cabin on each side at night. Then the challenge got extreme as one of them peed at the German camp during Swiss Day in the fountain and in the middle of the main square. I was surprised, disgusted, and a little bit impressed. Mostly I wondered why they had it in for the German camp. Then I learned that the German staff had played multiple tricks on the French, including moving their beds into their main square. I then understood why the French camp's Eiffel Tower had been toppled and encased in plastic wrap.

We made fun of this international rivalry when we staged an evening program. Dressed in lederhosen, I attacked Michele from Basilicata dressed as a Roman senator during the sack of Rome. We fought on the dock, and Michele always ended up in the lake as a running joke to end the evening. He then confessed that this was how he did his laundry. Tiziana, dressed as Cleopatra, also ended up in the lake, tossed in by the Roman senators. She asked me, "That counts as a shower, doesn't it?"

Many of the campers followed the staff's lead, and hygiene began to slip. Most of them showered in their swimming trunks, and when they didn't even do that, I tried to get them to swim or sauna. Little Rinaldo didn't bring his swimming trunks and didn't change his clothes in days. Fortunately, he was staying only one week. My own son, eight-year-old Lorenzo, had simply stopped changing his clothes, despite Katy's pleas. Perhaps he believed he was doing her a favor by not getting all his clothes dirty, but he managed to ruin all his clean clothes by packing his wet towel and swimsuit with them.

Rather than single out kids, I made a silly announcement at lunch to the whole camp: "You know, Martina, I feel so liberated here without my mamma and papà to watch over me. I've decided not to bathe or change my clothes the whole time I'm here. I'm not even going to change my socks or underwear. That's how free I am here!"

The kids laughed at how ridiculous and disgusting this was. Martina responded jokingly, "Yuck! You have to change your clothes!" And all the campers agreed in unison. I relented. Lorenzo thought it was so funny that someone wouldn't change clothes, but then he (and others) appeared in the same clothes the next day. Katy saw Lorenzo the next day in the same pants that he'd worn numerous times, and she begged him to change. He brushed her off cheerily, "It's OK, Mom, because I also wore them to bed as pajamas!"

THERE WILL BE BLOOD . . .

COMPLETE DARKNESS ENVELOPED THE ITALIAN CAMP AT NIGHT, since we had no electricity in the cabins or any lights on the paths. When the moon was full, we had a night light, but a new moon meant utter blackness. The darkness allowed us to see the fireflies, the North Star, and foxfire. Armed with just a flashlight, the brave campers ventured to the light of the bathroom for a late night pee but never further. No lights in the cabins meant the campers went to sleep when the sun set.

One night past dusk I was painting on a name tag for my son Lorenzo in the arts and crafts hut, which has bright fluorescent lights. When I turned off the switch to go back to my cabin, I realized I had no flashlight. After my eyes adjusted, I couldn't even see my hand in front of my face. I reasoned that I either had to sleep in the craft cabin or crawl back to my bed on my hands and knees so I wouldn't run into a tree. I reached into my pocket for my cell phone to call one of the staff to save me. The light of the touch pad gave off just enough light to guide me home.

Luca, the head cook, had one of the few tiny cabins with electricity, and it stood within reach of the business office's Wi-Fi and just five feet from the water's edge. He had spent his savings on a big-screen TV, which he squeezed through the door. It filled up half of his little cabin. A serpents' nest of electrical cords allowed the precious signals to travel to his state-of-the-art video game system.

In spite of my encouragement to participate in our evening programs, he preferred blasting away monsters with a Gatling gun after the stress of feeding seventy hungry kids and staff, who always had advice on how to keep the risotto perfectly *al dente*. While we were chasing kids into cabins, the light from his monitor showing the carnage of monster blood glimmered across the ripples of the lake.

The staff house had light as well. The counselors sneaked out of their cabins filled with sleeping kids to socialize with the other staff late into the night. I made a rule that one counselor must remain in each cabin and vetoed the old rule that allowed no counselors in the cabins as long as two of them on night watch wandered by the cabins to make sure all was quiet. Some staff protested, but this new rule also fulfilled my goal of ensuring the staff would sleep since some stayed awake until three o'clock every night and then looked like the living dead the next morning.

Fabio had a new proposal to take advantage of the sunlight by adjusting all of our clocks at camp to be one hour later. Lucrezia argued that it wouldn't give us any more light. "There's only a certain amount of light, so it's ridiculous to change our clocks. We should just change the schedule so we get up an hour earlier." Rather than sounding the wake-up bell at eight o'clock, we should sound it at seven, she reasoned. That way we wouldn't confuse everyone who came to camp, and the business office wouldn't accidentally make mistakes with the buses.

"No way!" Giulio protested. "I will never agree to waking up at seven o'clock."

Lucrezia argued, "But it will still be seven o'clock even if your watch says eight o'clock!"

"That's OK," Giulio continued, "but I will not wake up at seven A.M.!"

I worried that this early schedule gave us too much time in the evening, but then I figured that we could tell scary stories that would keep them in their cabins. Nowadays, though, telling gruesome ghost stories of real-life dismemberment and cannibalism isn't generally considered to be good pedagogy. The French camp, who used the site right before us, set the tone by proclaiming "*pas de violence!*" (no violence!).

Letizia agreed with this "peace and love" philosophy, but I argued, "That's all fine in real life, but can't we have some fun?" At our staff meeting, I announced that the kids, especially the boys, wanted mock fighting. "We need more blood," I declared, and the staff didn't know how to take this proclamation from the boss.

I explained that when the counselors duel during the gladiator battles, we needed blood spraying on the sand and limbs chopped off, just like Monty Python. "No, no!" protested the assistant cook, who had worked at the French camp earlier in the summer. She flashed the peace sign and warned, "No violence!"

We staged a comic version of the assassination of Julius Caesar, but some of the staff resisted my call for at least some blood on his tunic. All the senators were captured and brought in front of the campers to be put on trial. My son Leo, who was just seven, yelled, "*Tagliateli la testa!*" (Cut off their heads!).

Matteo looked at me and joked, "Dario, what are you teaching him?" Well, at least he conjugated the verb correctly. I used this as an example and said we could have done a funny skit at the end, but the peaceniks won out.

When one of our counselors, Anastasia from Athens, planned a special Greek Day, I realized we were not going to be able to build a Trojan horse or reenact the Battle of Thermopylae, but couldn't we at least break some plates when dancing to bouzouki music? Anastasia agreed with the plan, but the kitchen wouldn't let us destroy any plates.

"Don't you have just a couple of old plates we can smash?" I asked.

"They're all old plates," Luca replied. "Do you want to eat off of napkins for the rest of the session?"

The Greek Day went well, despite the lack of Spartans. Fortunately Luca and Giacomo in the kitchen made it up to me by supplying us with plenty of baggies full of watered-down ketchup for the upcoming gladiator battles. The kids constructed armor and shields out of cardboard, duct tape, and tin foil. The best gladiators from each cabin donned safety goggles and battled each other with Styrofoam swimming noodles. The emperor Nero watched on and demanded more combat, more carnage!

After the campers' gladiator competition, Gianni, the giant counselor, challenged six counselors to a battle to the death. While the other counselors prepared for the combat on the beach, Gianni grabbed the numerous blood packs, and I sat back and watched the gladiator battle unfold. The giant held a pack in each hand, and each time he grabbed an enemy counselor, the red juice spurted over their cardboard armor and soaked into the sand.

The comic butchery on the beach delighted the kids, especially when our tiny daughter, Stellina, grabbed one of the Styrofoam swords and impersonated the big kids by swinging it furiously. She brought down the goliath Gianni as cheers erupted from the bloodthirsty crowd. Even Letizia grudgingly admitted that bloodletting can be funny.

Tiziana wouldn't stop there, of course, but wanted to take this show on the road. For the Italian presentation at the end of International Day, she wanted six of the largest male campers, supplied with armor, shields, and helmets made from the best cardboard covered with tinfoil, to reenact a Roman blood bath at the Colosseum in front of all the language villages. While the other camps traditionally performed a medley of ethnic waltzes that turned into modern, sexy discotheque raves, Tiziana envisioned full-contact gladiator battles as our representation of Italian culture—and the more violent the better. Other counselors and I had doubts; Tiziana was annoyed we didn't understand that gladiators were one of the main draws for young boys to attend Italian camp.

I had to be the spoilsport and nixed the idea that I feared would result in dozens of blood packs coating the stage in gore, and the red liquid being sprayed into the audience. I pointed out, "I just don't think the acts that follow would appreciate dancing on a blood-soaked stage."

Tiziana complained that I was scared sellout who didn't trust her. "Yes, you're right. I don't trust you," I confirmed.

"Well you shouldn't," she agreed but declared that we would show the other camps what Italian camp is all about. Despite my protests and concern from Letizia, Tiziana began secret training rituals for the performance, which involved a lot of shouting and "art classes" in which the teenaged boys made intricate armor and weaponry. She promised that it would all go fine and they didn't need safety glasses since the armaments were just foam swords covered in cardboard. I conceded since the campers unanimously wanted an intense show rather than my idea of reenacting the comic opera *Barber of Seville*.

When the big day came, the six gladiators, who came from the oldest and most macho cabin, marched on to the stage oiled up and ready for combat. In front of hundreds of spectators, the warriors pledged to a haughty Caesar dressed in a toga and wearing a laurel wreath around his curls, "*Ave Imperator! Morituri te salutant!*" (Hail

Emperor! Those who are about to die salute you!). The crowd went quiet, perhaps confused by this bit of Latin and why everyone from Italian camp was screaming for the battle to begin. Tiziana blasted "O Fortuna" from *Carmina Burana* over the speakers, and the deafening Latin lyrics inspired the gladiators to fight to the death, but of course in an artfully choreographed scene with some even teaming up to double stab the weaker warriors.

They didn't hold back, as I had hoped. I worried they could truly hurt each other, as these testosterone-fueled boys took their roles seriously. The victims died with drama as half of the crowd cheered and the rest sat stunned by the performance. As Caesar gave the thumbs-down signal to the last gladiator to kill the others off, I nervously looked over at one of my bosses, Denise, worried that I'd finally be fired. She normally held back any judgment, but now she seemed genuinely horrified by the mock battle when the theme of the year was something like "peace and love." The last gladiator, after stabbing his adversary numerous times to finish him off in a painful death, gave a full-throated shout of victory at the end and ripped off his armor to show his sweaty, oiled-up body, much to the delight of the girls. I breathed a sigh of relief that no one was hurt; maybe I wouldn't lose my job after all. One of the older alumni later thanked me, "I don't know how many more of those uncomfortable sexy dances of thirteen-year-olds I could take!"

Other evening programs followed this gory lead, so soon we had an evening of the plague and all the bizarre cures used in Venice to stave off impending death. We reenacted the "bonfire of the vanities" in Florence, when Botticelli and others burned their artwork because the crazy charismatic friar Girolamo Savonarola called for an end to the decadence of the Renaissance and a return to good old-fashioned self-flagellation. We staged Dante's *Inferno* with its nine circles of Hell and delightfully gruesome scenes of suffering counselors.

In preparation for one of the evening programs, I asked Lucrezia where Tiziana was. "Oh, she just ripped out Gianni's heart and is eating it."

I didn't understand what Lucrezia was talking about but was somehow unsurprised. I noticed the kids and counselors laughing uproariously as they exited the dining hall, where Tiziana had reached into Gianni's chest as part of a skit, pulled out a giant tomato, and chomped on the dripping red mess. The kids loved the gory scene and didn't seem the slightest bit scared.

Instead, they were now all joyously terrified of zombies. I didn't understand why witches, skeletons, werewolves, vampires, and all the other evil creatures of the night weren't scary anymore. Tiziana began the rallying cry, asking everyone, "What do we do when the zombie apocalypse comes?"

"*Sopravvivere!*" (Survive!), the campers yelled back.

Tiziana confided to me that she and the other counselors had been plotting a hypothetical situation in the staff house of "Who would we sacrifice? Who would die first?" She then confessed to me that she was truly terrified of zombies, even though she knew they weren't real. "When I'm walking on the paths alone, I often think about what I'd do if a zombie came after me right now," she confessed. Then she pointed to the roof of one of the cabins that could be easily accessed with a little jump. Apparently zombies are so clumsy that they couldn't jump up there after her.

I told Luca about Tiziana's silly plans, but he said he had already worked out a much more elaborate plan about how to survive. "If fast zombies come after us, we don't have chance. If slow ones come at us, you can't just use a gun because you'll eventually run out of ammunition. That's why you need a shovel or some other blunt instrument."

My wife, Katy, asked him, "You know that zombies aren't real, right?"

"Yes, of course," he replied and then hesitated. He explained that theoretically zombie-like symptoms could happen from certain drugs or diseases that could turn into an epidemic. He just wanted to be prepared.

Luca criticized Tiziana's plan of climbing on the roof as just a temporary solution. During the zombie apocalypse, he intended on going to Split Rock Lighthouse along Lake Superior because "it's cliffs on one side, so when they come from the land you just need the correct weapons." Luca explained that zombies are not smart, so you can sometimes distract them. "I saw a film once about a zombie that was resurrected but just wanted to mow his lawn," Luca explained. "The ones we have to look out for, though, are the 'magical zombies.' Every part of them must be destroyed. Even if you cut off a hand, it will come after you. That's why you have to burn them."

I pointed out that this was like the "cleansing fire" that Dante described in *Purgatory,* and why they burned heretics at the stake in medieval times.

"Umm, sure, if you say so," Luca replied. "Well, if the robot invasion happens, the zombies don't stand a chance."

When the mail came, one of the usually even-tempered counselors received a zombie survival guide, and Tiziana got her shipment of pure-white contact lenses. She was planning a scary evening program based on the Black Death in Italy in which she'd have pure white eyes without irises or pupils.

To set the stage for this evening of undead terror, Luca prepared a demonic menu to get the kids in the mood to be frightened. He roasted whole chickens but put no silverware on the table, so we had to pull the poor birds apart with our hands. The campers got into the spirit and tore the legs off the delicious chickens. Dessert was Jell-O in brain-shaped molds, and the kids dug in, happily disgusted. To gather the dishes, the kitchen staff stumbled into the dining hall dressed as zombies. Then Tiziana, as one of the "quick" zombies, with one white eye and lots of stage blood, leaped out, hungry for brains, like any self-respecting member of the undead. I wondered if my push for more blood had been misguided, but the kids screamed with joy as the chaos of a zombie apocalypse began.

That night when the total darkness of a new moon fell, the kids huddled in their beds; no one dared leave their cabins. As I walked through the woods, I saw an entire stump glowing green and recognized it as enchanted foxfire. I took a chunk to show the kids in their cabins, but they screamed when I knocked. I was worried I'd get whacked with a shovel, but they let me in when they heard my voice. I showed them the phosphorescent crystals, and they gazed in awe. They now believed in magic. This mysterious substance somehow calmed them, and they slept soundly, as if pixies, not zombies, watched over their dreams.

COFFEE EMERGENCY

EARLY IN THE MORNING AT ITALIAN CAMP, I WAS AWAKENED BY cries of "Dario! We have an emergency!" I scrambled out of bed, assuming that some kid had lopped off his hand or a bear had made a tasty treat of a plump little camper. Would I have to put some severed limbs on ice as we rushed someone an hour to the closest clinic? Zeta, the assistant dean, said grimly, "I don't think we're going to make it."

"What?" I panicked. "What on earth happened?"

"We're out of coffee."

I laughed, but she wasn't kidding about the severity of the situation. The previous director had purchased a $5,000 espresso machine, and the blissed-out staff worked nonstop. Typical of Italian machines—from Maseratis to Moto Guzzis—they are unstoppable when working well, but they require constant tinkering. I often had to take time away from the campers to adjust the espresso machine for maximum strength and perfect *cappuccini*. A functioning espresso machine had a direct relationship to the happiness of the staff. Now with just a week of camp left to go, we had a crisis at Italian camp: no coffee.

Although this may seem melodramatic and overblown, I

announced the situation at the staff meeting. The counselors emitted a collective gasp, and panic ensued. One of the new counselors admitted that she had slowly upped her dosage each day to "at least eight espressos to keep me going. Not having any more just isn't going to work; they'll eat us alive." Michele confessed that he had far surpassed eleven espressos each day.

"That can't be good for you," I asked worriedly.

"I feel as strong as Hemingway," he replied.

"Eleven coffees in a day is pretty normal," Paola said nonchalantly.

Tiziana skipped the tiny Italian demitasse cups and just filled a giant twenty-four-ounce Wonder Woman mug with espresso a few times a day. "I was wondering why my stomach was always so upset," she said. Either that or it was the massive amounts of raw garlic Tiziana was ingesting for energy, while everyone kept clear of her and her interesting new scent.

I asked Luca, the head cook, how we'd reached this point of no coffee. He was not addicted to caffeine, in spite of my efforts to feed him a double cappuccino every morning and make him one of us. He was not too concerned with the lack of coffee and told them to just get over it. He said he had originally ordered plenty of beans to last the entire session, but the staff had drunk so much that he had had to reorder. The distribution center hadn't brought any last time, so "We'll just have to wait until Thursday."

"That's two days away!" a dumbfounded lifeguard responded. "How are we supposed to survive?"

I dug through the kitchen pantry and discovered an old bag of coarse-ground McGarvey coffee for drip makers. One of the Mr. Coffee makers had already been destroyed when an Italian put milk through the system rather than water to try to make a *cappuccino*.

With only our fancy Italian espresso machine left, I tried using the McGarvey coffee, which strangely lacked any smell or taste whatsoever. "Ugh, I'm not drinking that sock juice," Francesco complained and immediately dumped it down the drain.

"No, no, no!" Michele put his foot down. "You may drink such brown water in America, but we will not at Italian camp." Even the desperate American staff had higher standards now and couldn't stomach this "flavorless sewage."

With a useless espresso machine, the whole camp was put on hold. We'd reached that crucial point during the summer when the energy and confidence of the campers surpassed that of the staff. I'd noticed that the rancid smell of dead mice in the staff house had seeped into the counselors' clothes like stale cigarette smoke, but they were indifferent. They'd do anything to get away from the kids, even lounge in the staff house on smelly sofas filled with mice corpses.

This must be an acquired immunity, I decided after stepping into one of the cabins where the stench of dirty socks and wet towels had won this group the dirtiest cabin award. Since the coffee had run out, I'd noticed that the counselors weren't so forceful about making the campers shower every other day but settled for an occasional dip in the lake. Still, one of the eight-year-olds complained after going to the bathroom right before dinner, "Now I have to wash both hands."

Seeing the camp's slow slide into squalor after just a day, I heeded the advice of Zeta: "Dario, you need to do something about this now!" I hopped into the car and zoomed to town in search of fancy coffee in the north woods of Minnesota. Finally, the third town I visited had a large grocery store and incredibly had passable Italian espresso beans. Salvation was in sight.

When I returned to camp, the staff didn't waste any time. In an effort to crush the caffeine headaches, two pounds of ground espresso beans were gone within hours. The mood changed almost instantly. The end of camp was no longer seen as impossible but as imminent, and the staff were now ready for action. They fired up the sauna and reimplemented a regular bathing schedule. Sergio discovered a decomposed mouse in the staff house, scraped most of it off the floor, and poured bleach on the rest. He left the mess for Letizia to clean up. Then another source was discovered: the most popular La-Z-Boy in the staff house housed an entire family of mice that had gone to their maker. Exhausted staff had lounged in the chair, too tired to care about the stench. Now, though, Zeta rallied the staff, and they carried the gargantuan chair outside and to the dump.

The cook ran to tell me that a shipment of ten pounds of Italian roast espresso beans had just arrived by special courier. Even though we had only two days left, I was sure the Italians could make a good dent in this supply. With this surge of artificial energy, the tide had turned in favor of the staff.

THE END OF CAMP?

IT LOOKED LIKE JUST ANOTHER MIDNIGHT THUNDERSTORM, A great light show, the kind that thrills the kids at Italian camp with bright flashes and big bangs followed by a soaking rain. We woke up to a jungle-like mist off the lake. This time, though, the howling wind instantly knocked out the power. The horizontal rain pushed through the screens and soaked my bed. I woke up wet and tried to shut the casement windows in my cabin but could barely hold on to the handles.

Letizia called to see if we should wake the kids and take shelter in the cinder-block bathhouse. Out my window I saw a downed pine amid flying sticks but couldn't hear other trees falling over the surging gusts. No one should go anywhere, I said, we should hunker down and wait it out.

I could see flashlights pop on in the other cabins, and one beam pierced the darkness and walked outside. I found out later this ray of light came from Salvatore, who tried to walk to the staff house to check the storm conditions. I yelled to get back inside, but the deafening wind drowned out my voice. He saw the falling trees, recognized he didn't need a weather report, and ran back to his cabin.

After the twenty-minute front subsided, Scott, the caretaker, knocked on my door. "Dario, you need to come out here. I think this might have been a tornado." I scrambled through the debris and dozens of downed trees scattered around to check on the kids' cabins. Everyone was quiet now and sound asleep, and the cottages had minimal damage. Scott told me that when daylight came, no one should help out wounded wildlife. I asked would we really have hurt animals coming to us for help? Just then, we heard a fox wailing in the woods.

Luca's little cabin, three feet from the shore, had gotten the brunt of the storm's wrath. The neighboring cabin, fortunately vacant, was raised four feet off its foundation. Trees had fallen all around Luca's cabin, but I could hear him snoring happily inside. I shone my flashlight in to see if he was indeed all right. "What?" he mumbled groggily, obviously annoyed that I had woken him. He looked around at all the destruction, perhaps a bit disappointed that he had slept through the apocalypse.

He got dressed, and I shined my flashlight for him as he climbed over several trees to escape his cabin. He put on his tricorn hat, then pulled something out of his pocket that crumbled into little pieces. "Darn, that's the Pop-Tart that I wanted for later!"

I let everyone sleep except for Lucrezia, whom I dragged out of bed to help me assess the damage and make a plan. The biggest tree in camp, a two-hundred-year-old white pine had fallen next to the dining hall and spared it, but the little kitchen where we did cooking activities had been crushed by five basswoods. The wind had scattered the aluminum canoes around camp like confetti. One was wrapped around a tree, and another had flown fifteen feet into a stand of cedars.

Scott saw the damage and sent a text to his wife that he might have to close up for the season. Was this the end of camp? He couldn't even say if we'd be able to come back next year.

Luca told me, "Dario, we can't keep the kids here. We have to evacuate."

Lucrezia and I considered our options. We could barely walk to the dining hall under and over fallen trees. The dirt road would be too risky for a few dozen kids to navigate. Besides, Scott told us, power lines were down across the asphalt road into town.

"We have to go out by boat," Luca concluded. We didn't have a pontoon boat or even an outboard motor. I imagined us escaping camp in a flotilla of canoes, paddling through the waves to the public landing on the other side of the lake. But then where would we go?

The German camp generously offered their spare cabins. Once Vale awoke, she pleaded, "Please don't make us sleep with the bats again." Then I thought about it. Would this be admitting defeat? The parents would pick up their kids from German camp, rather than Italian, and who knows if they'd ever come back? Had the storm conquered camp? Besides, how would we even fit all their giant suitcases and sleeping bags into the canoes, and what would happen if a canoe tipped and all their clothes sunk to the bottom?

Once the sun rose above the horizon, the inspector from the Minnesota Department of Health suddenly appeared out of nowhere. "Wow, I had to climb over trees to get in here. It looks like you have a situation here." I assumed that he was here to officially shut us down once and for all.

Luca calmly explained to him that because of the storm, this really wasn't the best time for an inspection. Incredibly, he understood and agreed to stop back in a couple of weeks on a normal day when we could actually get to the dining hall.

Now that the first rays of light showed us how many trees had fallen, we reassessed the situation. No one was hurt, and the pizza oven was untouched. Whew! It seemed most wise to stay put since leaving the site could be far more dangerous than staying. In an emergency, we could still get a camper out of our site in about twenty minutes by paddling across the lake. We would tough it out at camp, but Lucrezia wisely pointed out that we'd need large amounts of coffee. When the administrators in Bemidji asked if we needed anything immediately, I responded, "Chain saws, water, and, well, coffee." Charlotte from the French camp arrived an hour later, parked a quarter mile away because of all the fallen trees, and crawled under Norway pines and hopped over live power lines with two giant thermoses of coffee for the counselors, who were now slowly waking up to the destruction.

Now we could face the rising sun, which cast a light on dozens of downed trees. Charlotte and Luca then set off in a canoe to haul bottles of water back to camp from her car. Scott set up a generator to feed electricity to one of the wells, so we at least had one set of working bathrooms. The administrators ordered more water and portable toilets to be delivered once the roads were cleared and to tide us over until the electric company restored full power.

As the campers slept an extra hour, we worried they'd be terrified by the devastation once they had woken. "This is so cool!" little Giovanni exclaimed. We had strung caution tape around potentially dangerous areas, which made it all the more exciting. Obviously, this was an adventure to them, not a tragedy. I had prepared a speech to try to allay their fears and convince them that they had lived through a "historic storm, the worst ever seen at Italian camp," but this just got them more excited about how great this was. I told them that we might be without electricity for several days, but Giovanni pointed out, "We don't have electricity in the cabins anyway, so who cares?"

They asked each other if they had been scared by the storm, but almost all of them claimed they hadn't been. Neva, the counselor from Bergamo, admitted that she was terrified, but the kids said they liked the danger. Giovanni said, "My mom doesn't like it when I ride my mountain bike because she thinks I'll get hurt, but I'm a kid! I'm supposed to get hurt." The nurse wasn't thrilled to hear that. We continually steered the kids away from the danger zones.

Then came the lumberjacks. One muscular young man strutted by without a shirt over his tanned body. His low-hanging pants thumbed their nose at gravity. A strap over his shoulder counterbalanced a giant chain saw off his front, and a dripping gas can hanging off his back. With his hands free, he slowly smoked a cigarette, unconcerned that a spark could ignite the fumes at any time. Lucrezia, Letizia, and I watched in awe. Lucrezia uttered, "I think that's the sexiest thing I've ever seen."

As the chain saws dug into the dozens of trees and Bobcats rammed away the wreckage, we led the kids to the one building we could access, the lodge. The cooks had lugged in a cold breakfast of apples, cheese, and water, and we ate as the machines buzzed in the background at this once serene camp. Meanwhile, Luca and the other cooks desperately tried to save food from the coolers. They cleaned all the debris from the kitchen and struggled to think how they could possibly feed an entire camp without power or running water. They grilled bratwurst for lunch, and we ate off paper plates. Ten-year-old Domenica said, "It's so nice that the cooks get a break since they work so hard."

The lumberjacks as well worked nonstop. The highlight was a middle-aged "climber" with spiked shoes and a tree-climbing belt who scaled a giant red pine that leaned precariously over the staff house. With his chain saw he chopped all the limbs off to give his ring belt a clear path to the top. I asked if he had forgotten his helmet and protective glasses, but he said they just got in the way. He whistled happily, "I've been doing this since I was eight, and that was forty years ago!" We had roped off the tree since we didn't know if it would just fall, but he said that with all the weight from the branches he had cut off gone, the tree should hold his weight. Once on top of the tree, nearly seventy feet in the air, he chopped six-foot sections, which fell to the ground with a thud. I asked his buddies what would happen if he fell. "Well . . . we'd all go and have a beer for him." One of the lumberjacks turned to the awed campers and advised, or perhaps challenged them, "Please, kids, don't try this at home."

We told the campers that the show was over, because we still had Italian lessons. Giovanni replied, "Man, I wish a tree would fall on that part of the day!"

By afternoon, the lumberjacks had cleared the road all the way to the dining hall. They thought they would just have to remove a half-dozen pines, but Scott lost count after one hundred downed trees. The woodsmen had brought a rumbling wood chipper, which shredded much of the debris. We struggled for an Italian word for this device until Neva realized that she had seen one of these in the film *Fargo,* in which the killer used it to dispose of his partner's dead body.

Lucrezia concurred, "Yes, this is how you get rid of Steve Buscemi."

After six days without power, we finally saw the lights come on. Scott said that we could stay after all and camp could continue. The counselors cheered that the kids could take showers rather than relying on the sauna to get clean. We realized what a luxury, not a necessity, electricity is.

Lucrezia pointed out, "It took surprisingly long—about forty-five minutes—for the Italians to remember that because we have electricity again, our espresso machine is working."

Strangely, living without electricity and running water had been a welcome challenge for the kids and would give them bragging rights when they saw their parents at the end of camp. One of the kids said, "If this happened at the German or French camps, they would have shut down!" Despite their bravery, when the kids heard thunder rumbling in the distance, they shuddered. We tried to assure them—and ourselves—that we could endure anything since we had just survived the biggest storm our camp had ever seen.

THE LAST DAY OF CAMP

"Why is Zeta's bicycle up in the tree?" my four-year-old child asked me as we walked to the dining hall past a mountain bike stuck high on a branch twelve feet from the ground.

"You'll have to ask her," I responded but knew that the pranks had just begun. Zeta instigated these practical jokes but thankfully left me out. Someone was obviously retaliating against her tricks. We had only two days left of Italian camp, and I worried that this revenge would escalate.

"How come you never play any tricks on us?" Zeta asked me.

I explained that if I started, the floodgates would open, and anyone would be justified in what they did in retaliation. I kept secret that I was keeping a journal of these dispatches from camp as my joke on all of them—even as I was worried that this exposé could finally get me fired.

The next morning, the Italian flag was on the ground, and Alceste's skimpy Speedo was flying high from the flagpole. Alceste, a counselor from Le Marche, laughed and took this as a compliment, assuming that the women were impressed by his skintight swimsuit. "Everything's funny as long as it happens to someone else," little Italo pointed out.

The following morning, all of Matteo's clothes—suitcase and all—ended up on the floating raft in the middle of the lake. He was not amused, especially since he wore the Gucci and Prada summer fashions. In fact, he refused to work until someone retrieved his clothes for him. While not admitting he had done this prank, Alceste began sleeping in a hidden location to avoid a vendetta.

Suspicion of being pranked swept through the camp at the end of the summer. Even though we had fixed our beloved espresso machine, the lethargic staff complained about throbbing headaches. Many wanted to take naps rather than run through the woods with the kids. Something was wrong, so I inspected the bags of beans used to fill the coffee grinder and my theory was correct: we were drinking decaffeinated coffee. At our staff meeting, I jokingly laid the blame for this terrible trick on Letizia, who was the most responsible and trustworthy counselor.

"Oh, I think I might have done that by accident," she confessed. "I was just trying to help."

"Should we burn her car in revenge?" I joked.

"Yeah! Then she'd know what it feels like to drink decaf," Luca said.

Letizia reminded us that she doesn't have a car—she's always one step ahead of us.

"Besides," Luca added, "if you burn her car, you can't go any higher with pranks."

Marina had a better idea, "Let's just wait until she's asleep and cut off all her hair."

I cautioned the counselors to go easy on the pranks. "No more underwear up the flagpole!" I decreed. We didn't want the campers to start playing tricks on each other, since they wouldn't know when to stop. It was too late, though, because the kids had clued into these jokes and wanted in on some of the fun. Zeta's cabin of high school girls raided a boys' cabin, took all their wet towels, and left them in a heap blocking their door. The Italian counselor of that cabin, Sergio, was incensed about this "very destructive action" and demanded an apology.

Zeta told me, "He's outraged about that? You should have heard what the girls wanted to do! I talked them down to just piling up their towels."

The damage was done, and Sergio demanded justice. I calmed Sergio down, saying that perhaps Italians are more mature than we Americans, who don't know when to stop. He agreed that this must be an example of the cultural innocence of Americans.

I then learned that the older boys in Sergio's cabin had been pranking the older girls for weeks. One trick was tying string to the handle of the girls' screen door and running the taut line all the way to the boys' cabin. They waited for Sergio to fall asleep, and they tied the string to his wrist. Each time he tossed and turned at night, the girls' screen door opened and slammed with no one there.

With each joke, the boys left a pear as their "signature." One day, the boys sneaked into the girls' cabin and left a pear but didn't do anything. The girls went crazy searching for some stunt but found nothing. One of the boys told me later, "That was the best prank of all."

Amid this paranoia about inevitable pranks, I tried to keep everyone busy with activities on the last day. Sergio took a few of the older kids on a nature walk, while Zeta and another counselor took a group on a bike trip around the dirt roads of the camp.

The rest of the counselors prepared for our daily staff meeting. Lucrezia rushed into the meeting and announced that some boys had just raided the girls' cabin and thrown their mattresses on the roof. Of course this was in retaliation for the girls entering the boys' cabin and throwing their shoes on their roof, which was likely revenge for something else. Zeta told everyone to calm down.

I went to investigate the mattress situation before a possible thunderstorm arrived. I was interrupted by the counselor Beppe, who said that a group of boys were butchering frogs behind the kitchen.

I asked Elisabetta to deal with the roof wars, while I ran behind the dining hall. Sergio greeted me happily as he stood over three very pleased high school boys who had a clear plastic bag filled with bouncing frogs. The kids had a large cutting board on the ground with a shiny cleaver next to it and were preparing for the next step.

"Stop!" I said. "What on earth are you doing?"

Sergio responded happily, "We caught some frogs on our nature hunt and are going to make a snack."

"No, you're not," I insisted.

"You always want us to do multicultural activities. Well, this is what the French do, and we eat frogs in Italy too. They're very nutritious."

"You can't just eat any old frog out of the swamp," I said.

I then noticed that one of the cooks, Assunta, was actually overseeing this scene. She said, "It's the same as if they caught a fish and cleaned it. What's the difference? In fact, these are healthier than ones you'd find in a store. Well, if you could find frogs in a store."

"I catch and cut up frogs all the time back in Montana," one of the campers told me. "They're tasty."

I was beginning to wonder if this was a prank on me. Why would these kids want to eat frogs? Why would the cook allow campers to use a sharp knife, especially a cleaver? Would Sergio then want to roast cats, which he claimed was an Italian delicacy? Still, I couldn't risk it. "I'm sorry," I said. "This is a terrible idea and I can't . . ."

Just then Zeta skidded her mountain bike to a stop by us and said, "Two kids took off on the bikes. I think they want to go all the way around the lake."

We initiated a missing camper search and took all the kids into the dining hall as all available staff set out to find the two boys on bikes. Letizia hopped on a bike to go after them, and eight other counselors searched by car. The camp caretaker phoned the neighbors to keep on the lookout. We were a dozen miles from the nearest town in one direction and forty miles in the other direction, with cornfields and lakes in between.

I prepared to call the police in town to see if they could help. Just then Letizia wheeled into camp with the two fugitives. Incredibly, the two boys were proud that they had almost made it around the lake and were oblivious to the headache they had caused us. One of them realized, "Oh, I suppose we should have told someone what we were doing."

Somehow this emergency created a sense of unity. The staff and campers in the dining hall cheered that no one was lost. The pranks and resulting vengeance seemed to be forgotten, or at least forgiven, for the moment. Sergio and the three boys came out of the kitchen, licking their lips. "Mmm, the frogs were *deliziosi!*" a camper said.

"I thought I told you not to . . ." I started to say but realized it was pointless by then.

"Assunta the cook did everything for us," Sergio said proudly, "just as you asked. Now these boys can survive out in the wilderness on frogs."

I sighed and hoped they would survive until we sent them home on the bus first thing the next day.

The giant coach bus arrived down the dirt path, weaving through the woods and scraping some paint on protruding branches; the bus driver was crabby. He was already late and wasn't pleased that the campers were in no rush to get on board to go home. In fact, they desperately tried to ignore the bus, which represented the end of their adventure. They exchanged addresses in hopes of staying in touch forever. I knew that once they started to cry, we'd be here another hour. Lucrezia pointed out, "They cry when they arrive, and they cry when they leave." Finally, Nina convinced all the staff to line up in a single file that led right to the door of the bus so the campers could give a hug to each counselor and climb aboard. Some of the kids were a bit awed by the giant Gianni at the end of the line. He acted awkwardly about hugging kids, so he shook their hands formally and gave out a hearty belly laugh: the last little prank of the summer.

Finally with the kids aboard, the bus pulled out, and the exhausted counselors wanted to collapse. Instead, we had to close down the entire site, which no one was ever motivated to do. We always discover numerous wet towels and swimsuits that somehow escaped from suitcases. Abandoned artworks—those precious crayon versions of the *Mona Lisa* on butcher paper, and pasta glued together to make Venus on the half-shell—were thrown into a box, only to be unpacked next summer (and then thrown out).

I asked the staff who planned on returning next summer, but Lucrezia stopped me by warning, "You should never ask right away who is coming back, because everyone is just trying to recover and swears they'll never do it again." To recruit them back, I should wait until the dark days of winter when the hot summer months at camp seem like paradise.

My wife, Katy, in the meantime, had packed up our three kids, Leo, Lorenzo, and Stellina, and completely filled the station wagon for the long drive home. As she was leaving, little five-year-old Stellina asked, "Papà, when can we come back to camp?"

ACKNOWLEDGMENTS

THE STAFF AND KIDS AT ITALIAN CAMP MADE THIS BOOK POSSI-ble with their energy, humor, and dedication. They made great stories, and many let me use their real (fake) names: Alceste, Alpina, Angelina, Assunta, Beppe, Bonifacio, Carlo, Carlotta, Cesare, Elisabetta, Eva, Fabio, Francesco, Gabriella, Gaetano, Giacomo, Gianni, Giulio, Irene, little Leo and Lorenzo, Liliana, Linda, Livia, Luca, Lucio, Luigi, Luisa, Maggia, Marina, Martina, Matteo, Michele, Nico and Nico, Nina, Paola, Paolo, Roberto, Rosa, Rosella, Salvatore, Scott, Sergio, Silvia, Stellina, Tea, and Vale.

A special thanks to my readers: Lucrezia, Letizia, Tiziana, Zeta, Murasaki, and my brother Michael.

Of course this all began with the great indoctrination into the wilderness at YMCA camps: Icaghowan, Camp Christmas Tree, and Menogyn. Phil Gilbert and BJ Kirk led us on the trip of a lifetime in northern Wisconsin.

François Fouquerel and Teresa Belisle took a chance on me as a counselor at the American camp in France. None of this would have been possible without the enduring support of the fantastic Concordia Language Villages (and far too many people to thank here!). The German and French villages deserve recognition for their patience with the sometimes-too-proud Italian village. *Merci, Katy, und vielen dank,* Karl.

The fabulous University of Minnesota Press staff, especially Erik Anderson, brought this book to press. Thanks also to Kristian Tvedten and Heather Skinner, who gets the word out like no one else.

Most of all, thanks to my kids, Eilif, Otto, and Astri, for coming to camp, and to Katy for putting up with my annual retreat to the north woods for the past ten years.

Eric Dregni is associate professor of English at Concordia University in St. Paul. He is the author of many books, including *Minnesota Marvels, Midwest Marvels, In Cod We Trust: Living the Norwegian Dream, Never Trust a Thin Cook and Other Lessons from Italy's Culinary Capital, Vikings in the Attic: In Search of Nordic America, By the Waters of Minnetonka,* and *Let's Go Fishing! Fish Tales from the North Woods,* all published by the University of Minnesota Press. During the summer, he is dean of Lago del Bosco, the Italian Concordia Language Village. He lives in Minneapolis.